## The R. Cotter Drug and Medicine Manf'g Co.
(WM. GINNUTH.)

# WHOLESALE DRUGGISTS.
—DEALERS IN—

### DRUGS, PATENT MEDICINES, DRUGGISTS' SUNDRIES,
*Toilet and Fancy Articles.*

### SHOW CASES AT MANUFACTURERS' PRICES.

PROPRIETORS OF

Cotter's Chill Cure, Cotter's Headache Pills, Cotter's Sarsaparilla, Cotter's Cherry Cordial, Cotter's Cholera Specific, Cotter's New Liniment, Cotter's Liver Pills, Etc.

P. O. Box No. 327.          HOUSTON, TEXAS.

---

## ALF. CHIMENE,
Manufacturer of and Dealer in

# FURNITURE, CARPETS, MATTINGS,
Parlor Sets, Window Shades,

**No. 73 Main Street,** - - - **HOUSTON, TEXAS.**

---

## GEORGE KIDD,
# FRUIT AND PRODUCE COMMISSION MERCHANT,
*120 Main Street, HOUSTON, TEXAS.*

---

## JOHN ACHENBACH,
MANUFACTURER OF

# FINE BOOTS AND SHOES,
—AND DEALER IN—

### LADIES', GENTS' AND CHILDREN'S BOOTS, SHOES, &C.
*STORE AND FACTORY.*

103 Congress St., opp. Court House,     HOUSTON, TEX.

---

## *M. MELLINGER & BRO.*
STAPLE AND

# FANCY GROCERS.
IMPORTERS AND DEALERS IN

### WINES, LIQUORS, ALES,
*AND PORTER,*

**89 and 91 Prairie St., HOUSTON, TEX.**

**PROMPT ATTENTION PAID TO ALL ORDERS.**

J. J. SCHOTT, *Galveston.*      F. H. COLBY, *Houston*

## SCHOTT & COLBY,
### DRUGGISTS,
86 MAIN STREET, HOUSTON, TEX.

— DEALERS IN —

Drugs, Medicines, Perfumery, Toilet Soaps and Mineral Waters.

**AGENTS FOR HOUSTON OF J. J. SCHOTT & CO.'S PREPARATIONS.**

PRESCRIPTIONS A SPECIALTY, DAY AND NIGHT, AT ALL HOURS.

---

# P. H. GALLIGHER,

## ❖ GROCER ❖

*No. 72 Main Street,*    HOUSTON, TEXAS.

---

## L. T. NOYES,

— DEALER IN —

### *Guns, Pistols, Hardware,*

**TINWARE, CUTLERY, FISHING TACKLE,**

— AND —

### House Furnishing Goods.

MECHANICS' FINE TOOLS A SPECIALTY.

HOUSTON,  - - - - - -  TEXAS.

General Agent for Texas of the

**DIEBOLD SAFE AND LOCK CO., AMERICAN POWDER CO., ÆTNA POWDER COMPANY AND YALE & SARGENT TIME LOCKS.**

# The First Texas Cook Book

# The First Texas Cook Book

*A Thorough Treatise on the Art of Cookery*

With Forewords

By David Wade and Mary Faulk Koock

EAKIN PRESS ★ Austin, Texas

1883

Originally published by
The Ladies Association of
The First Presbyterian Church, Houston, Texas

Texas Sesquicentennial Collectors Edition
From Facsimile of the original

Copyright © 1986
By Eakin Publications, Inc.

Published in the United States of America
By Eakin Press, P.O. Box 23066, Austin, Texas 78735

ALL RIGHTS RESERVED. No part of this book may be reproduced in any form without written permission from the publisher, except for brief passages included in a review appearing in a newspaper or magazine.

ISBN 0-89015-518-6

# Foreword

As an apostle of the art of great food orchestration, I applaud Eakin Press for its penchant in publishing anew *The First Texas Cook Book*. All Texans and anyone interested in the wonderful world of cooking should add this treasure to their library. Not only is this a document of the people of early Texas and their culture, but it showcases some of the finest approaches to food chemistry and imagination that I have seen.

This book confirms what I have always expressed about cooking, that the three most important ingredients of any good recipe are love, patience and butter. Certainly for these early Texans cooking was a labor of love as it required so much more time. Their patience had to be expanded when struggling with the kitchen tools of 1883. You can read just a few pages and you will see that almost every recipe was baptized in butter.

I will admit to dispassion when first I received this publication. Later as I read through it, I was compelled to my kitchen to test recipes and other kudos found in the work. I found that the simple method for making macaroni pasta is superb. The blueprint for negotiating a salad-style mustard from scratch cannot be improved. I suggest that you try the stuffed hard cooked deviled egg recipe that incorporates butter and other primitive trappings. Like me, I am sure that you will express exclamations of praise. Check the approach for making good coffee and the substitute for milk. Even they knew that the addition of one and one half biscuits dissolved in water and added to a lemon pie filling would keep it from separating.

You know, I have decided that my great Texas grandparents were pretty smart folks. I only wish that I could have spent a week or two in one of their kitchens. Since time machines have yet to be invented, I will have to settle with my copy of *The First Texas Cook Book*. I hope you will too.

Good living and
*Bon Appetit*
DAVID WADE

# Foreword

How well did the families of Texas dine more than a century ago? If you accept the recipes of this first Texas cook book published in 1883, they dined very well indeed!

The volume, identified as a "thorough treatise on the art of cookery," contains 721 recipes and eighty household aids in twenty-five sections. Seventy-two contributors, forty-seven of them from Houston, include one man who submitted a recipe for "Yacht Pie." His tongue-in-cheek recipe suggests that "the more ladies you have on board, the more onions should be used."

Many recipes show that the women of one hundred years ago favored the use of wine and spirits in their cooking. One of the recipes for making mincemeat included "four pints white wine, one pint brandy." And a recipe for making vinegar included "three quarts of whiskey."

Today's reader will be pleased and amused by names given many of the dishes such as "Kiss Pudding" and "A Nice Plain Plum Pudding" and "Very Nice Way to Poach Eggs." Also provided was folksy advice such as "old fowls are best for soup" and "spinach requires good washing and close picking." One recipe for cornfield peas suggests the first step to be "go to the pea-patch early in the morning and gather the peas, take them home in a split basket." An admonition continues: "take them in the left hand and gouge them out with your right thumb until it gets sore, then reverse hands. Look the pea well in the eye to see its color . . ."

Much of the language in the book definitely dates it. The yolk of an egg was always spelled "yelk," as it was still spelled in many parts of the country in the early parts of the twentieth century. "Sally Lunn," not found on today's supermarket shelves, is defined as "a teacake slightly sweetened and raised with yeast, baked as biscuits or in a thin loaf and eaten hot with butter."

Since the "Art of Cookery" has been so important in my life, I am delighted at this bit of Texana culinary, I am enthralled at the simplicity and ingenuity of these recipes of a century and a sesqui-century ago.

My favorite recipe from page 38 is "Stuffed Veal."

MARY FAULK KOOCK

January 1986

# Introduction

The Reverend Mr. E. D. Junkin was in the third year of thirteen years he would be pastor of the church in 1883 when the women of the First Presbyterian Church of Houston published their *Texas Cook Book*.

The Church, organized in 1839, three years into Texas statehood, was located on the north side of Capitol Avenue between Main and Travis Streets. This first Texas cookbook was "edited" by the church's Ladies Association, which was five years old on the date of publication.

In his *A Brief History of the First Presbyterian Church,* published in 1939, S.C. Red says that Mrs. George W. Kidd, then the president of the association, "was largely responsible for the entire undertaking," though her name appears nowhere in the book. *The Texas Cook Book* is a singular tribute to Mrs. Kidd and any others responsible for it. The anonymous writer of the Preface, later called the book "the first enterprise of its kind in our state."

In 1880, Houston had a population of 16,513 and may have reached twenty thousand three years later when the book was published. The city's first telephone had been installed five years earlier. The barroom of the Capitol Hotel, whose site was later occupied by the Rice Hotel, had become the first place in Houston to be lighted by electricity just a few months before the book was published. Ten railroads entered the city by 1883, when Houston had a mile of plank "paving," eighteen blocks of graveled streets and two blocks of stone pavement. The rest, as a rule, was dirt, or in Houston's case much of the time, mud.

This volume is from a facsimile of the original and so contains the typographical errors from the first hand-set copy. The original contained a number of pages of advertising from Houston merchants not included in this edition. The price of the book, "on sale at all booksellers," was $1.50.

The book closes on a rather somber, but practical note, with household suggestions from a wide variety of problems from "a sure bed bug exterminator" to "how to prevent mildew on preserves."

*Not much use: no times or temperatures.*

# PREFACE.

As many of the very excellent cook books published contain receipts not suited to the requirements of our climate, and, as far as we know, no complete treatise on the subject of cookery has been published in our latitude, it has seemed well to supply this deficiency.

The receipts given have been obtained from our best housekeepers and cooks; are the results, not of theoretic cookery, but of practical testing and approval. As such, we offer them to the public.

The first enterprise of its kind in our State, we ask for it a *fair trial*. In the TO-DAY of competition, we are well aware that only because of its *merits* shall our Cook Book prove a success, and knowing these, we fearlessly accept the conditions.

HOUSTON, TEXAS, 1883.

# The First Texas Cook Book

# LIST OF CONTRIBUTORS.

| | | |
|---|---|---|
| Mrs. A. C. Allen, | . . . . | Houston, Texas. |
| " T. C. Armstrong, | . . . | Galveston, " |
| " Rob't Archer, | . . . . | Houston, " |
| " A. A. Adey, | . . . . | " " |
| " E. C. Atkinson, | . . . | " " |
| " Abbott, | . . . . | " " |
| " A. J. Burke, | . . . . | " " |
| " Lilly Barrett, | . . . . | " " |
| " James Bailey, | . . . . | " " |
| " E. C. Blake, | . . . . | " " |
| " George Bastian, | . . . | " " |
| " G. H. Bringhurst, | . . | " " |
| Miss Baxter, | . . . . | Shreveport, La. |
| Mrs. Rob't Brown, | . . . | Navasota, Tex. |
| " S. E. Byers, | . . . . | Houston, " |
| " M. H. Bozeman, | . . . | Hempstead, " |
| " Jane Connell, | . . . | Houston, " |
| " Wm. Christian, | . . . | " " |
| " J. L. Cunningham, | . . . | Bastrop, " |
| Miss Julia Crow, | . . . | Austin, " |
| Mrs. Jas. Converse, | . . . | Houston, " |
| " H. L. Carmer, | . . . | Chappell Hill, " |
| " A. W. Davis, | . . . | New Orleans, La. |
| Miss Agnes L. Dwight, | . . . | Chicago, Ill. |
| " Dunovant, | . . . | Eagle Lake, Tex. |
| " Forman, | . . . . | Richmond, Ky. |
| Mrs. E. R. Falls, | . . . | New Orleans, La. |
| " R. M. Fenn, | . . . . | Houston, Tex. |
| " T. J. Girardeau, | . . . | " " |
| " G. A. Gibbons, | . . . | " " |
| " T. W. House, | . . . | " " |
| " C. S. House, | . . . | " " |
| " J. R. Hutchison, | . . . | " " |
| " W. A. S. Haynie, | . . . | " " |
| " C. M. Hurd, | . . . . | " " |
| " J. Hill, | . . . . | Bastrop, " |

| | |
|---|---|
| Miss L. Hutchison, | Houston, Tex. |
| Mrs. O. H. Hutchison, | " " |
| Hon. J. C. Hutchison, | " " |
| Mrs. F. W. Henderson, | " " |
| " W. J. Hancock, | " " |
| " E. D. Junkin, | " " |
| " J. W. Jones, | " " |
| " Dixon Lewers, | Palestine, " |
| " A. L. Lacey, | ———— |
| " J. R. Morris, | Houston, Tex. |
| " G. A. McDonell, | " " |
| " M. A. McDowell, | Bastrop, " |
| " N. A. Milton, | Houston, " |
| " G. E. Miller, | " " |
| " C. T. McLelland, | " " |
| " L. C. Noble, | " " |
| " L. M. Noble, | " " |
| " Fannie Noble, | " " |
| " B. D. Orgain, | Bastrop, " |
| " E. O'Donoghue, | Chicago, Ill. |
| " Parker, | Louisiana. |
| " J. A. Peebles, | Hempstead, Tex. |
| " John D. Rogers, | Galveston, " |
| " E. Reid, | Corsicana, " |
| " J. D. Sayers, | Bastrop, " |
| " Jas. W. Stacey, | Houston, " |
| " D. C. Smith, | " " |
| " Judge Thompson, | Virginia. |
| " F. C. Usher, | Houston, Tex. |
| " E. H. Vincent, | " " |
| " M. E. Warren, | " " |
| Miss Annie Williams, | " " |
| Mrs. Rob't Wilson, | " " |
| " Weems, | " " |
| " R. H. White, | Hempstead, " |
| " R. E. C. Wilson, | Houston, " |

# INDEX.

### SOUP.

Vegetable—Tomato—Very Nice Chicken Soup—Potato—Tomato Soup, No. 2—Egg Balls for Soup—Beef Soup—Crab Gumbo—Chicken Gumbo—Chicken Soup, No. 2—Mock Turtle—Split Pea—Asparagus—Mushroom Ochra Gumbo—Filé Gumbo—Mutton—Green Corn—Gumbo Filé—Okra Gumbo—Oyster Gumbo—Noodles—To Brown Flour, Etc.................................. 17 to 22

### FISH.

Fricassee Fish and Tomatoes—Fish Chowder, No. 1—Fish Chowder, No. 2—Barbecue Fish—Shrimps with Mayonaise Sauce—Potted Shrimps—Codfish—Codfish with Eggs—Codfish Balls—Codfish on Toast—Baked Red Fish—Fried Fish—A Nice Way to Prepare Canned Salmon—Baked Fish—Baked Crabs—Crab Omelet.... 23 to 26

### OYSTERS.

Oyster Salad—To Fry Oysters—To Cook Oysters—Oyster Soup—Broiled Oysters—Oyster Omelet—Scalloped Oysters—Oyster Loaf—Scalloped Oysters—Oyster Omelet........................................................... 27 to 29

### MEAT.

Rules for Boiling Meat—Boiled Leg of Mutton—Cooking Cold Meats—Broiled Sweet Bread—Pickled Brains—Kidney with Tomato Sauce—Broiled Kidney—Chicken and Ham Pie—Croquettes—Potted Beef—Yacht Pie—To Broil Quail—To Smother Fowls—Croquettes of Poultry—A Nice Way to Cook Chicken—Roast Turkey—Turkey Dressed with Oysters—Boiled Turkey—Scalloped Ham—Pigs Head—Ham Croquettes—Deviled

## INDEX.

Ham—Hog's Head Cheese—Boiled Ham—Baked Ham—Melton Veal—Economical French Dish—Potted Meat—A Nice Way to Prepare Beefsteak—A Nice Way to Prepare Steak—Beefsteak Smothered with Onions Nice way to Cook a Round of Beef—Beef á la Mode—Veal Collops—Spiced Beef—Broiled Venison Steak—Veal Croquettes—Stuffed Veal—Veal Loaf Veal Cutlets with Oysters—Breaded Veal—Veal Stuffed with Oysters—Calf's Head, No. 1—Calf's Head, No. 2—Sweet Breads Broiled—Sweet Breads Fried—Wine Stew—A Good Stuffing for Turkey or Fowls.................. 30 to 40

### SAUCES FOR MEATS.

Sauce for Fish—Dressing for Crabs or Boiled Fish—Drop Dumplings for Meat—Caper Sauce—Drawn Butter Sauce—Dressing for Salads, Meats, Salmon, Etc.—Cream Sauce—A Good Mayonnaise Dressing—Apple Vinegar—Vinegar—Pickle for Tongues or Ham—Common Mustard—Mustard Sauce—Worcestershire—Celery Sauce—Parsley Sauce...................................... 41 to 44

### HASH.

Fish Hash—Ham Hash—Hash—Baked Hash—Fried Hash—Pig's Head Hash.................................. 45 to 46

### CATSUPS.

Tomato Catsup, No. 1—Pepper Catsup—Tomato Catsup, No. 2—Green Tomato Sauce—Tomato Soy—Tomato Catsup, No. 3—Tomato Catsup, No. 4—Tomato Catsup, No. 5—Green Tomato Soy—Cucumber Catsup, No. 1—Cucumber Catsup, No. 2...................... 47 to 49

### SOUR PICKLES.

Chow-Chow, No. 1—Higden Salad—Mangoes—Pepper Mangoes—Peach Mangoes—Chili Sauce, No. 1—

## INDEX.

Pickles—Cucumber Pickles—Chow-Chow, No. 2—Chili Sauce, No. 2—Yellow Pickle—Chili Sauce, No. 3—Green Tomato Pickles—Spiced Tomatoes............ 50 to 53

### SWEET PICKLE.

Tomato Sweet Pickle, No. 1—Cucumber Sweet Pickle—Green Tomato Sweet Pickle — Watermelon Sweet Pickle—Peach, No. 1—Peach, No. 2—Plum—Tomato, No. 2—Sweet Pickle—Peach, No. 3—Pickled Peach, No. 4—Pickled Peaches, No. 5—Green Tomato Pickle.. 54 to 56

### SALADS.

Potato Salad, No. 1—Potato Salad, No. 2—Potato Salad, No. 3—Lobster Salad—Cabbage—Chicken, No. 1—Chicken, No. 2—Chicken, No. 3—Chicken, No. 4—Chicken, No. 5—Egg Salad—Chicken, No. 6.......... 57 to 59

### SLAW.

Hot Slaw—Cold Slaw, No. 1—Cold Slaw, No. 2—Cold Slaw, No. 3............................... 59 to 60

### BREAD.

Light Bread, No. 1—Bread, No. 2—Fried Bread, Nos. 1 and 2—Tea Bread—Sally Lunn—Flannel Cakes, No. 1—Flannel Cakes, No. 2—Sour Milk Batter Cakes—Mississippi Batter Cakes—Batter Cakes—Beat Biscuit—Waffles, No. 1—Waffles, No. 2—Waffles, No. 3—Rice Muffins—Flour Muffins—Griddle Cakes—Corn Muffins—Muffins or Sally Lunn—Muffins—Biscuit, No. 1—Maple Biscuit—Drop Biscuit—Graham Biscuit—Biscuit, No. 2—Buttermilk Biscuit—Corn Batter Cakes—Bread Cakes—Rice Bread—Corn Bread—Indian Bannock—Hominy Bread—Corn Cakes—Nice Biscuit—Graham Gems—Genuine Scotch Bread—Split Rolls—Plain Bunns—Rusk—Short Cake—Parkin—Bunns—

INDEX.

Salt-Rising Bread — Graham Bread — Potato Yeast Bread—Milk Sponge Bread—Boston Brown Bread, No. 1—Boston Brown Bread, No. 2—Boston Brown Bread, No. 3—Light Bread—Salt-Rising Bread.............. 61 to 71

### YEAST.

Yeast Cakes, No. 1—Yeast Cakes, No. 2—Potato yeast, No. 1—Yeast Cakes, No. 3—Dry Hop Yeast—Yeast That Will Not Sour—Potato Yeast, No. 2—Yeast......... 72 to 74

### VEGETABLES.

Vegetables--Cabbage a la Cauliflower--Corn Fritters--Green Corn Fritters—Corn Oysters—Baked Tomatoes, No. 1—Stewed Tomatoes—Baked Tomatoes, No. 2—Fried Tomatoes—Stuffed Tomatoes—Fried Tomatoes, No. 2—To Broil Tomatoes—Tomatoes Baked Whole—Sweet Potatoes—Fried Sweet Potatoes—Very Nice Sweet Potatoes—Baked Sweet Potatoes, No. 1—Baked Sweet Potatoes, No. 2—Baked Sweet Potatoes, No 3—Boiled Sweet Potatoes—Boiled Irish Potatoes—Fried Irish Potatoes—Saratoga Potatoes—To Boil Irish Potatoes—Mashed Irish Potatoes, No. 1—Roasted Irish Potatoes—Fried Irish Potatoes—Mashed Irish Potatoes. No. 2—To Cook New Potatoes—A Nice Breakfast Dish, No. 1—A Nice Breakfast Dish, No. 2—Squash—Boston Baked Beans—Boiled Onions—To Fry Ochra—Celery—Parsnip Fritters—Parsnip Stew—Spinach—To Prepare Egg Plant—Scalloped Parsnips—Baked Egg Plant—Turnips – Asparagus—Succotash—Ochra and Tomatoes—To Cook Green Peas—Boiled Hominy—Rice Omelet—To Cook Beets—Beans—Cashaw—To Cook Cornfield Peas........................................ 75 to 84

### OMELETS AND EGGS.

An Omelet—Plain Omelet—Egg Omelet—Parsley and Eggs—Stuffed Eggs, No. 1—Stuffed Eggs, No. 2—

INDEX.

Stuffed Eggs, No. 3—Poached Eggs—A Very Nice Way to Poach Eggs—Baked Eggs—Hard Boiled Eggs—Soft Boiled Eggs—Fried Eggs—Scrambled Eggs—Pickled Eggs.................................................... 85 to 87

### SIDE DISHES.

To Make Macaroni—Macaroni with Cheese—Macaroni Pudding to be Eaten with Meats—Welsh Rarebit—A Nice Breakfast Dish—A Nice Relish for Supper—A Nice Way to serve Cheese.................................... 88 to 89

### COFFEE, TEA AND CHOCOLATE.

Coffee—Mock Cream for Coffee—Dripped Coffee—Good Coffee—Mock Cream for Tea or Coffee—Chocolate, No. 1—Chocolate, No. 2—Tea............................ 90 to 91

### PIES AND PASTRY.

Good Pie Crust—Puff Paste—Pie Crust—Lemon Pie, No. 1—Lemon Pie, No. 2—Lemon Custard Pie—Lemon Pie, No. 3—Silver Pie—Lemon Pie, No. 4—Lemon Pie, No. 5—Orange Puffs—Lemon Puffs—Irish Potato Custard—Lemon Custard—Buttermilk Custard, No. 1—Buttermilk, No. 2—Lemon Custard—Jelly Custard—Cream Custard—Citron Custard—Apple Custard Pie—Cocoanut Pudding—Mock Mince Pie—Peach Cobbler—Apple Pie, No. 1—Apple Pie, No. 2—Jelly Pie—Strawberry Short Cake—Green Apple Pie—Orange Pie—Washington Pie—Sweet Potato Pie—Mince Pies—Cracker Pie—Molasses Pies—Irish Potato Pie—Transparent Pie—Mince Pie Without Meat or Apples—Mock Mince Meat—Apple Meringue—Prime Meringue—Sweet Potato Pie, No. 2—Cocoanut Pie—Molasses Pie—Mince Meat, No. 1—Mince Meat, No. 2—Mince Meat, No. 3—Mince Meat, No. 4—Mince Meat, No. 5...................... 92 to 101

## PUDDINGS.

Kiss Pudding—Chocolate, No. 1—Chocolate Pudding, No. 2—Chocolate No. 3—Chocolate, No. 4—Chocolate, No. 5—Cottage Pudding—Cottage, No. 2—Chocolate, No. 6—Snow, No. 1—Snow, No. 2—Plain—A Nice Plain Plum Pudding—Boston—Plum, No. 1—Corn—Delmonico—Custard—Poor Man's—Corn Starch, No. 1—Sallie Mason—Quaking, No. 1—Black Cap—Sailor's Duff—Orange, No. 1—Transparent—Plum, No. 2—Original Pudding—Cocoanut—Rice, No. 1—A Very Fine Pudding—Tapioca and Apple—Tapioca, No. 1—Rice, No. 2—Ginger—Yankee—Buttermilk, No. 1—Buttermilk, No. 3—Rice, No. 3—Delicious Pudding, No. 1—Plum, No. 3—Tapioca, No. 2—Corn Starch Pudding, No. 2—Bird's Nest Pudding—Bread and Apple—Lemon—Sponge Cake Pudding—French—Carrot—Molasses—Delicious, No. 2—Plum, No. 4—Cherecoke—Apple Tapioca—Orange, No. 2—Webster—Cheap Currant—Quaking, No. 2—Apple—Estelle—Queen of Puddings—Lemon Roll—Brown Bettie—Excellent Sauce for Pudding—Pudding Sauce—German Sauce—Wine Sauce for Puddings—Confederate Sauce—Sauce for Pudding—Pudding Sauce—Eris Pudding ........................ 102 to 115

## CAKES.

Fruit Cake, No. 1—Fruit, No. 2—Fruit, No. 3—Rich Fruit—Fruit, No. 4—Black—Fruit, No. 5—Pecan Fruit Cake—Fruit, No. 6—Fruit, No. 7—White Loaf, No. 1—Gold Cake—White Loaf, No. 2—Yellow—White Loaf, No. 3—White Loaf, No. 4—Silver—White Loaf, No. 5 White Cake Without Eggs—Mountain, No. 1—Angel Cake—Angels' Food, No. 1—Angels' Food, No. 2—Angels' Food, No. 3—Angels' Food, No. 4—Snow Cake, No. 1—Snow, No. 2—Yellow Loaf—White Sponge—

## INDEX.

Sponge, No. 1—Sponge, No. 2—Sponge, No. 3—Sponge, No. 4—Sponge Cake Roll—Good Sponge—Sponge, No. 5—Sponge, No. 6—Cheap Sponge—Sponge, No. 7—Lady Fingers—Water Sponge—Delicate Cake—Delicate Cake for Tea—Nuns' Puffs—Apple—Feather—Corn Starch, No. 1—Pound Cake, No. 1—Pork—Seed—White Fruit or Cocoanut—Pecan, Hickorynut—Soft Ginger Cake—Superior Ginger Cakes—Ginger Cake—Boston Ginger Bread—Ginger Bread—Hard Ginger Bread—Pound Cake, No. 2—Corn Starch, No. 2—Cup, No. 1—Cup, No. 2—A Good Cake—Tea Cakes—Cookies, No. 1—Cookies, No. 2—Jumbles—Cookies Without Eggs—Snappish Ginger Snaps—Ginger Cookies—Ginger Crackers, No. 1—Ginger Snaps—Ginger Crackers, No. 2—Soda Cake—Cocoanut Tea Cake—Crullers, No. 1—Crullers, No. 2—Crullers, No. 3—Crullers, No. 4—Crullers, No. 5—Doughnuts—Ammonia Jumbles—Wafers—Mountain, No. 2—Snow, No. 3—Spice, No. 1—Marble, No. 1—Marble, No. 2—Marble, No. 3—Marble, No. 4—Spice, No. 2—Marble, No. 5—Neapolitan, No. 1—Neapolitan, No. 2—Jenny Lind, No. 1—Jenny Lind, No. 2—Imperial—Ice Cream Cake—Dolly Varden—Watermelon—Buttermilk—Washington Cake—Washington Pie—Lemon Jelly, No 1—Lemon, No. 1—Lemon, No. 2—Lemon Jelly, No. 2—Rolled Jelly Cake, No. 1—Rolled Jelly, No. 2—Coffee Cake, No. 1—Coffee, No. 2—Coffee, No. 3—Cocoanut, No. 1—Cocoanut, Cake, No. 2—Chocolate, No. 1—Cocoanut Chocolate Cake—Orange—Chocolate, No. 2—Chocolate, No. 3—Chocolate, No. 4—Cream Cake, No. 1—Cream Jelly—Cream, No. 2—Cream Puffs, No. 1—Cream Puffs, No. 2—Cream Custard Cake—Custard Cake, No. 1—Custard Cake, No. 2 .................. 116 to 142

INDEX.

### ICING AND FILLING FOR CAKES.

Boiled Icing—Chocolate Icing, No. 1—Cold Frost Icing—Chocolate Icing, No. 2—Icing made with Gelatine—Icing made with Gelatine—Lemon Jelly, No. 1—Cream Filling for cakes—Lemon Icing for Cakes—Lemon Jelly, No. 2—Golden Sauce .................... 143 to 144

### BRANDIED FRUITS AND PRESERVES.

Brandy Grapes—Brandy Peaches, No. 1—Brandy Peaches, No. 2—Brandy Peaches, No. 3—To Can Peaches—Peach Chips—Can Peaches—Peach Marmalade—Ripe Tomatoe Preserves—Preserved Peaches, No. 1—Spiced Raisins—Citron—Preserved Tomatoes—Preserved Peaches, No. 2—Water Melon Rind Preserves—Fig Preserves—Fig Jam—Apple Jelly, No. 1—Grape Jelly—Wild Plum Jelly—Apple Jelly, No. 2—Wild Plum Jelly, No. 2—Wild Plum Jam—To keep Green Grapes........ 145 to 152

### FANCY DISHES.

Banana Fritters—Orange Fritters—Apple Fritters—Plain Fritters—Cheese Fritters—Apples for Tea—Steamed Apples—Oranges Sliced—Apple Compote—Apple Jam—Snow Flake, No. 1—Floating Island—Apple Cream or Snow—Apple Custard—Compote of Apples—Ornamental Dish—Apples with Jelly, for Tea—Snow Flake, No. 2—Frosted Peaches—Apple Float—Apple Snow—Solid Custard—Lemon Meringue—Boiled Custard—Custard—Snow Custard—Pine Apple Cream—Russian Cream—Fruit Salad—Spanish Float—Whip Syllabub—Spanish Cream, No. 1—Spanish Cream, No. 2—Charlotte Russe, No. 1—Charlotte Russe, No. 2—Charlotte Russe, No. 3—Whipped Cream—Tipsey Squire—Meringues—Vanity—Nondescripts, No. 1—Egg Kisses, No. 1—Egg Kisses, No. 2—Trifle—Aurora—Nondescripts, No. 2—Wine Jelly—Ambrosia, No. 1—Ambrosia, No. 2—Snow—Syllabub—Floating Island—Corn

## INDEX.

Starch Blanc Mange—A nest of Eggs—Preparation of Figs for Market—Macaroons—Sugar Candy—Butter Scotch—Cocoanut Candy, No. 1—Chocolate Caramels, No. 1—Chocolate Candy—Chocolate Caramels, No. 2—Cream Chocolate Drops—Cocoanut Candy, No. 2—Peanut Candy—Prauliens—Black Crook Candy—Cocoanut Candy, No. 3—Cocoanut Candy, No. 5—Cream Candy, No. 1—Cream Candy, No. 2—Molasses Candy—Chocolate Cream Drops—Cream Nuts ................ 153 to 166

### WINES AND DRINKS.

Dewberry Wine—Blackberry Wine, No. 1—Blackberry Wine, No. 2—Scuppernong Wine—Blackberry Wine, No. 3—Mustang Grape Wine—Blackberry Cordial, No. 1—Blackberry Cordial No. 2—Blackberry Cordial, No. 3—Ginger Beer—Cream Nectar—Imperial Lemonade—Milk Punch .................................................... 167 to 169

### ICES.

Lemon Ice—Lemon Sherbet—Italian Cream—Frozen Custard—Frozen Peaches—Cocoanut Cream—Frozen Whipped Cream—Strawberry Cream—Wine Sherbet—Strawberry Ice—Water Melon Ice—Gelatine Ice—Wine Ices—Milk Sherbet ................................. 170 to 172

### MISCELLANEOUS RECEIPTS.

Measures for Housekeepers—To Prevent Mildew on Preserves—Japanese Cleansing Cream—Cologne Water—Extracting Odor from Flowers—To Remove Scorches—To Remove Ink Stains from Cloth—To Remove Dampness—To Rid of Red Ants—To Polish Knives—For a New Pen—To wrap a Newspaper—For Frozen Plants—Hair Wash—To Remove Odor of Onions—Potatoes used as Soap—To Clean Matting—To make a Beefsteak Tender—To Dry Sweet Corn. A good Sprinkle for Plants—Liquid Glue—To Prevent Knives Rusting—American Cleansing Fluid—Bed Bug Destroyer—Cure for Burns—Cockroach Destroyer—A Sure Bed Bug Exterminator—

## INDEX.

To Prevent Flies Specking Picture Frames—To Clean Decanters—To Clean Kid Gloves—To Keep Insects from Bird-cages—Stove Polish—Blueing—Mildew, to Remove—To Remove Machine Grease—To Remove Stains from White Cloth—To Remove Mildew—To Remove Oil or Grease from Floors—To Remove Black Ink from Floors—To Sweep a Carpet—To Wash Flannels—Excellent Hair Wash—To Crystalize grasses—Crystalizing—Cough Syrup—Stew for a Cold—Sulphur for Diphtheria—Cure for Chronic Diarrhœa—To Relieve Neuralgia—Remedy for Sore Throat—Cough Mixture—Piles—A Sure Cure for Coughs and Colds—Relief for Whooping Cough, etc.—Cure for Earache—Cure for Nose Bleeding—Cure for Diarrhœa—To Stop Nose Bleeding—For a Felon—Bread and Milk Poultice—Remedy for a Burn—Remedy for a Sore—Remedy for Diarrhœa—Cholera Mixture—To Cure Toothache—Liniment—For Bowel Disorders—Cure for Dyspepsia—Worth Knowing—Remedy for Ague—Remedy for Ivy or Vine Poisoning—Head Wash—Simple Remedy for Three Dangerous Diseases—To Prevent Lockjaw—For Burns—For Chapped Hands—A Good Liniment—A Good Liniment—For Summer Complaint—Tomato Syrup—Beef Tea—Beef Tea—To Remove Ink Stains—To Clean Brushes and Combs—To Clean Brushes—Ink Stains from Matting—To Remove Blood Stains—To Clean Windows—To Clean Pots—Preventive for Asthma—Cure for Toothache—To Wash Blue Woolen Goods—To Remove Fruit Stains—To Destroy Cutworms in Gardens—Cleansing Woolen Clothes—Prickley Heat—To Clean Kid Gloves—To Remove Spots from Kid Gloves—Recipe for Blueing.................. 176 to 186

# SOUPS.

### Vegetable Soup.

Two turnips, two carrots, four Irish potatoes, one large onion, one parsnip, a few stalks celery or parsley. Cut all very fine; add a spoonful of rice; put the whole into three quarts of water; boil three hours. Strain the soup, return to the kettle and place over the fire; add a piece butter the size of a nut; stir the soup until the butter melts; add a little flour, let it boil, and then serve. Mrs. M. E. Warren.

### Tomato Soup.

To a gallon of rich broth made of fresh meat (veal is best) add five dozen tomatoes with skins on—if fresh tomatoes are not to be obtained, use one can of tomatoes. Let it stew steadily and slowly two hours in a well-covered soup-kettle; salt to taste, and strain through a colander. To a large tablespoonful of butter, rub in the same quantity of flour, add the soup and return to the fire several minutes. A slight flavor of onions may be added. Mrs. J. R. Morris.

### Very Nice Chicken Soup.

Put on four quarts of water, with two or three slices of old ham or middling. Let it boil sometime, then put in the chicken with the fat or skin taken off, a small onion chopped fine. Let it simmer until nearly done, then season with pepper, salt, parsley and thyme. Just before serving, add a pint of milk, with the yelk of an egg beaten in. Thicken with a tablespoonful of flour, with a lump of butter rubbed in.

Mrs. Judge Thompson, Va.

### Egg Balls for Soup.

Yelks of two hard boiled eggs, yelk of one raw egg; mix with a little flour, and roll into small balls.

### Potato Soup.

One quart milk, one stalk of celery, one small onion, four potatoes, boiled and mashed, one tablespoonful of butter, and one of flour creamed in. Add salt to taste. Put through a sieve, and serve in a hot tureen.

Mrs. Judge Thompson, Va.

### Tomato Soup.

Boil soup-bone four or five hours; remove meat and strain; add one small onion, chopped fine, three potatoes, one tablespoon of rice, one can tomatoes; season with salt and pepper, and boil one hour.

### Beef Soup.

Boil soup-bone two and one-half hours; after boiling one-half time add one tablespoon fine-cut cabbage, one medium size onion cut fine, two Irish potatoes cut fine; salt and pepper to taste; one teaspoon of flour made into a thin batter; add the latter when done; stir and cook a few minutes longer.

Mrs. M. E. Warren.

### Crab Gumbo.

Take one dozen crabs, boil thoroughly and pick out; two and a half quarts okra, chopped, and one large onion, also chopped; fry two-thirds of the okra with the onion; have a gallon of water in a pot, take two slices of ham, all the okra and two tablespoonfuls of rice, put into the water and boil down to a thick gumbo; this will take two or three hours; season to taste, and about an hour before ready to serve put in the crabs.

To make beef gumbo, use beef instead of crabs, and add a few tomatoes.

For chicken gumbo, fry a chicken brown and pick off from the bones, and use in place of crabs or beef, adding tomatoes as before.

Mrs. T. C. Armstrong, Galveston.

### Chicken Gumbo.

Fry a young chicken light brown; in another vessel fry a pint of young, tender ochra, cut fine; also cut fine two onions; put all in a porcelain kettle, add one quart of water, stew gently until done, and season with pepper and salt; a slice of good ham and two spoonfuls of raw rice added to the gumbo when it first begins to boil is a great improvement; simmer the whole three or four hours; serve with a separate dish of rice. If ochra cannot be obtained in sufficient quantity, thicken by adding a tablespoonful of dried sassafras leaves, pounded fine, mixed with a little of the gumbo and stirred into the whole. Gather the leaf buds of the sassafras early in the spring, dry, pound, sift and bottle them. The taste of the sassafras, however, is very disagreeable to some persons.

### Chicken Soup (No. 2.)

Cut up a large chicken, boil gently in three quarts of water, removing all scum; to half a gallon of soup add half a pint of rice, a few sprigs of parsley, pepper and salt to taste; boil till the chicken is done, add half a pint of sweet milk and one tablespoonful of corn-starch, stirred into a spoonful of butter. The chicken may be taken out and used for salad, or picked fine and added to the soup. Old fowls are best for soup. If the soup is for a sick person omit the butter. By making this soup without rice, adding milk or cream and oysters seasoned nicely, you have a most delicious soup.

### Mock Turtle Soup.

Boil the soup meat until very tender, then strain off the liquor, chop a small onion in very small pieces and fry a light brown; have a teacupful of browned flour, mix gradually in the liquor, put in the onion, a dozen allspice, one-half dozen cloves, four little red peppers, and season with salt and pepper. Let all boil together for half an hour; have two or three hard boiled eggs, chopped fine, in the tureen. Then when the soup is poured in the tureen add two tablespoons of wine, or the juice of one lemon.   MRS. T. W. HOUSE.

### Split Pea Soup.

Wash the peas, then put a teacupful of peas to a quart of water; add to this the soup meat, and let all boil for three or four hours; then take out the bits of meat and bone and strain the soup through a sieve.   MRS. T. W. HOUSE.

### Asparagus Soup.

Have the meat well boiled, strain off the liquor and add to it a bunch (or can) of asparagus and a little chopped celery; season with pepper and salt and boil for twenty minutes.

Mrs. T. W. House.

### Mushroom Soup.

Cut a knuckle of veal in large pieces and break the bones; allow to each pound a little less than a quart of water (milk is better), season with salt, half a dozen blades of mace and saltspoonful of cayenne. Boil until the meat falls to pieces, then strain into a clean soup-pot. Have ready a large quart of mushrooms, peeled and divested of their stems, put them into the soup, adding a quarter of a pound of butter divided into bits, each bit rolled in flour; boil until the mushrooms are tender, keep closely covered, have toasted bread in small pieces in the tureen and pour the soup over it.

Mrs. T. W. House.

### Ochra Gumbo.

Cut chicken and bacon in small pieces and fry brown, then take from the fire. Cut the ochra in small pieces and fry, then put all in a stew-pan with water sufficient for soup; season highly with pepper and salt.   Mrs. T. W. House.

### File Gumbo.

Brown a tablespoon of flour, put in a pot with quarter of a tablespoon of hot grease and two sliced onions, add to this a large slice of ham, also chicken, turkey or young veal cut up; fill the pot with boiling water and let the contents boil about two hours. A minute or two before serving add a pint of drained oyster liquor and 50 or 100 oysters, also a pod of red pepper. When ready to serve, after having poured the gumbo into a tureen, stir in a spoonful of filé. Have rice cooked dry to serve with it.

### Mutton Soup.

Boil a leg of mutton from two to three hours and season with salt and pepper. Just before serving add noodles made in this way. Beat one egg light, add a pinch of salt and flour enough to make a stiff dough, roll out in a very thin sheet, dredge with flour to keep from sticking, then roll up tightly, and beginning at one end shave off thin rings, drop into the soup and add a tablespoonful of summer savory rubbed fine.

### Green Corn Soup.

Six ears of corn, grate and boil the cobs in water enough to cover them. When done, remove the cobs and use the water in which they have been boiled to stew the grated corn, add one quart of sweet milk when ready to serve, letting it boil after the milk is poured in. Season with butter, pepper and salt.

### Gumbo Filé.

Take a large fat hen and cut in pieces as for frying; two large onions, cut very fine, and fifty oysters. After the chicken is cut up, soak in salt and water quarter of an hour, then rinse in clear water. In a deep pot, put one large tablespoonful of lard: as soon as it is hot add two tablespoonfuls of sifted flour, stirring all the time; as soon as it is a light brown put in the onions, and when they are brown, put in the chicken, with a little salt, and red and black pepper; stir well and frequently, and let simmer slowly for half an hour, then add half a can of tomatoes, and half an hour after, a quart of boiling water. Let boil harder. In half an hour more, add as much boiling water as will make a good tureen of soup, and let it boil slowly until ready to serve. About ten minutes before serving, add a tablespoonful of filé very slowly to prevent its getting into lumps. This is without oysters. When you use them boil the oysters and liquor together, then take out the oysters, put them in a dish and add them to the gumbo about a quarter of an hour before it is done; put the boiling liquor into the gumbo at any time, first skimming well, and put less water in the gumbo. Have a dish of boiled rice at table, and, when serving the gumbo, put a spoonful in each plate, and pour the gumbo over it.

Mrs. G. E. Miller.

### Okra Gumbo.

Prepare the chicken, onions, etc., as for gumbo filé. Have a quart of okra cut in fine rings, one can of tomatoes. Put in the lard, flour, onions, chicken, salt and pepper as for gumbo filé, then add the okra and tomatoes, and let it cook slowly for an hour, then add one quart of boiling water, and an hour afterwards add as much water as will make a good tureen of soup.

Both of these Gumbos require from three to four hours cooking, and frequent stirring to prevent burning.

Mrs. G. E. Miller.

### Oyster Gumbo.

Prepare the lard and onions the same. Put the liquor and oysters in a pot, and soon as it comes to a hard boil, skim, and pour in the lard and flour, and let boil for half an hour, and put in the filé and serve.

### Noodles for Soup.

Beat an egg, add a little salt, with flour enough to make a stiff dough; roll into a thin sheet, and fold it over and over, cut thin slices from the end and drop them into the soup.

To brown flour for soup, place it in the oven and let it brown, stirring constantly.

When carrots are used in soup they are better grated.

# FISH.

### Fricassee Fish and Tomatoes.

If the fish is large, cut in pieces, roll them in flour, season with pepper and salt; fry about half done; take up fish and set it aside. Scald and skin six large tomatoes, or more if they are small; cut a good sized onion fine, mix together and fry in butter, stirring to prevent scorching; pour over the tomatoes enough boiling water to make sauce for the fish; add wine if liked. Put the fish in the stew-pan, and simmer in the gravy until done. Spice may be added.

### Fish Chowder.

Take a small piece of pork, cut into squares, and put into the bottom of a kettle. Then take your fish (about three pounds will make a good sized chowder), cut it into pieces (larger squares than the pork), lay enough of this on the pork to cover well, then a layer of potatoes, next a layer of Boston crackers, split, on this, pepper and salt. Above this put a layer of pork, and repeat the order given above until the materials are all exhausted; let the top layer be buttered crackers. Pour on boiling water until covered, and cover the kettle; keep boiling half an hour. Five minutes before dinner, dredge well with flour, and pour on a pint of milk.

### Fish Chowder.

Take a fresh red fish, of three or four pounds, clean it well, cut in pieces of three inches square. Place in the bottom of your dinner-pot five or six slices of salt pork; fry brown, then add three onions, sliced thin, and fry those brown. Remove the kettle from the fire, and place on the onions and pork a layer of fish; sprinkle over a little pepper and salt, then a layer of pared and sliced potatoes, continuing to alternate layers of fish and potatoes till the fish is used up. Cover with water, and let it boil for half an hour. Pound six biscuits or crackers fine as meal, and pour into the pot; and, lastly, add a pint of cream or sweet milk; let it scald well and serve. (This is nice.)

### To Barbecue Fish.

Salt the fish well; put it in a baking-pan nearly full of water and boil until almost done, then pour off most of the water. Have ready a cupful of vinegar, black pepper and Worcestershire sauce and butter, melted together. Pour this over fish, a little at a time, until the fish is done. Sift a little flour over the fish between the times of putting on sauce and it will brown nicely.  Mrs. Jno. D. Rogers, Galveston.

### Shrimps with Mayonaise Sauce.

Boil three eggs *hard*, and a good sized Irish potato well-done; break open the eggs carefully, taking only the yelks; mash these and the Irish potato together, after which add a teaspoonful of sweet oil, the same of mustard, and vinegar to the taste. Have your shrimps ready boiled and picked, also three Irish potatoes boiled well done and sliced thin. When cool, lay all around your dish—first the young leaves of lettuce and then the sliced potatoes. Place the shrimps in the centre of the dish, with the whites of the eggs sliced thin and laid on them. Then pour over the mayonaise sauce; stick in the centre a fresh young head of lettuce, and you will have a delicious and nicely decorated salad for either dinner or supper.

A. W. Davis, New Orleans, La.

### Codfish.

Pick the fish in small pieces and soak some time in water to freshen it, then put it on the stove in cold water and let it simmer slowly, but not boil, as boiling makes it tough. Make a dressing of cream (or milk), seasoned with butter, pepper and salt, thicken with a little flour, pour over the fish and serve immediately. Some persons like boiled Irish potatoes placed in the dish with the fish, with the dressing poured over the whole.  Mrs. F. C. Usher.

### Potted Shrimps.

Melt butter in a pan and mix into it fresh picked shrimps, with ground mace and pepper to taste. Let them simmer, but not boil; when soft, fill shrimp pots with them and put aside to cool; when cool, spread unmelted butter on them and hold each pot before the fire a moment to give it a smooth appearance.

### Codfish with Eggs.

Pick into small pieces, soak well and simmer slightly. Place in a hot dish and pour over it drawn butter sauce, into which a number of hard boiled eggs have been sliced.

Mrs. Usher.

### Codfish Balls.

Prepare the fish in the same way as above, have ready Irish potatoes mashed and highly seasoned, into which work the fish carefully, make the whole into small cakes or balls and fry in boiling lard.

Mrs. Usher.

### Codfish on Toast.

Pick the fish in small pieces and put into cold water. Let it come to a boil, then strain in a colander, put into the skillet again with cold milk, season with butter and pepper, stir smoothly one tablespoonful of flour with a little cold milk, add and let it boil a moment and then serve on buttered toast.

### Baked Red Fish.

Dress it, wipe dry, rub well with salt and pepper inside and out. Fill the fish with stuffing made as for dressing fowls, only omit the onions, lard it well, sprinkle with a little flour, bake it in oven, put little water in the pan to keep from burning.

Mrs. A. J. Burke.

### Fried Fish.

After getting it ready to cook, have your lard boiling hot, roll the fish in salt, pepper, cornmeal, drop in lard flesh side down.

### A Nice Way to Prepare Canned Salmon.

Open the can and set it in a kettle of hot water; when well heated have ready a sauce of drawn butter, with a few sprigs of parsley chopped fine, also green pickles and the juice of one lemon; serve as soon as prepared; garnish with sliced lemon and parsley.     Mrs. C. S. House.

### Baked Fish.

Stuff the fish with mashed Irish potato and onion stuffing, then put in a deep pan and bake, cut up three or four large onions, put a tablespoonful of lard in a frying pan, as soon as hot add two tablespoons of flour; when brown put in the onions; as soon as they are brown add half a can of tomatoes and a pint of hot water, a few allspice, salt, black and red pepper; let cook for a quarter of an hour and pour over the fish about ten minutes before serving so as to flavor the fish.     Mrs. G. E. Miller.

### Baked Crabs.

Make a dressing as follows: One tablespoonful of made mustard, one teaspoonful of Worcestershire sauce, three tablespoons of sweet oil, cayenne pepper, black pepper and salt to taste and vinegar enough to mix well. Take the meat from one dozen large crabs or one can of crabs, put in a dish and pour over the dressing, mixing it well in, then add six soda crackers rolled fine, one raw egg, and mix all well together, then put into a dish or the shells, sprinkle over them cracker crumbs, put little pieces of butter on top and bake.
    Mrs. G. E. Miller.

### Crab Omelet.

Make a dressing as follows: One teaspoonful of mustard, half a wine-glass of oil, one wine-glass of vinegar, one teaspoonful of Worcester sauce, salt, red and black pepper to taste. Take the meat of a dozen crabs, or one can of crabs, beat up the eggs and mix all together, pour into a frying pan and cook like scrambled eggs, stirring all the time.
    Mrs. G. E. Miller.

# OYSTERS.

### Oyster Salad

Can of oysters, four eggs, one-half teacup of rich cream, heaping tablespoon of butter, one teacup of best vinegar, one teaspoon mixed mustard, cayenne and salt to taste, one-half small teacup of sugar. Mix these ingredients well—beat yelks and whites together, add other ingredients. Set the vessel containing this mixture into one of hot water; stir and boil until quite thick. When done, add one teaspoon celery seed, and rather more than a handful of crushed crackers—roll the crackers very fine. Pick your oysters nicely, and then pour this dressing over them.   Miss Forman, Cynthiana, Ky.

### To Fry Oysters.

Dry your oysters well, either in a colander or by spreading on a dry cloth. Take fine cornmeal and season well with salt and pepper; roll the oysters in the meal and fry at once in boiling lard while the meal is dry. Cook a light brown.

### To Cook Oysters.

Two quarts oysters, one quart fresh milk, one-half pound butter, one tablespoonful flour, one teaspoonful salt, one teaspoonful pepper, one egg. Rub the egg and flour together, and thin with a little of the milk. Mix the oysters, pepper and salt, and let them come to a boil, then add the milk; after this boils add the flour, egg and butter. Let all boil three minutes.

### Scalloped Oysters.

Take a baking dish, put in first a layer of oysters, sprinkle pepper, salt (if the oysters are not salt enough) and a little butter over them, then a layer of rolled cracker, next a layer of oysters, alternating thus until the dish is filled, having the top layer of cracker, with a little butter put in small bits over it. Bake only a few minutes, as oysters cook quickly. Serve hot in the dish in which they are baked.

Mrs. T. J. Girardeau.

### Oyster Soup.

One quart sweet milk, one quart oysters. Boil the liquor of the oysters with the milk; let it boil up twice and then add one tablespoon of butter. Use either crackers or flour to thicken while boiling; then add the oysters.

Mrs. G. A. McDonell.

### Broiled Oysters.

Dry the oysters in a cloth, salt and pepper them, and sift over a little finely powdered cracker. Broil quickly, and drop each one in melted butter. Serve in a hot dish garnished with parsley or horseradish.

### Oyster Omelet.

Chop fine twelve large oysters, beat six eggs and add a spoonful of flour, rubbed smooth in milk, season with salt, pepper and a little melted butter; fry in one omelet and serve hot.

Mrs. Lillie Barret.

### Oyster Loaf.

Take a fresh baker's loaf of bread (a hot one is best), cut out the top crust carefully, and remove the inside part, leaving the bottom crust and sides, butter the inside well and fill to the top with hot fried oysters, put slices of pickle over the top, put on the upper crust and keep until the bread is flavored with the oysters.

### Escalloped Oysters.

A dozen soda crackers rolled and a hundred oysters, drain the oysters, make a dressing with a dessert spoonful of mustard, one wine-glass of sweet oil, two of vinegar, one dessert spoonful of Worcestershire sauce, salt, red and black pepper to taste. Take a baking dish, sprinkle a layer of crackers, then put a layer of oysters, sprinkle in a little of the dressing, then another layer of crumbs, then oysters and dressing, until the dish is full, making the top layer of crumbs; on top put little pats of butter and put in the stove and let bake until a light brown.  MRS. G. E. MILLER.

### Oyster Omelet.

Make a dressing as above, drain the oysters and cut in half, put them in the dressing and let them stay half an hour, beat up the eggs very light, whites and yelks separately, have the frying pan very hot, put in the lard, then take the oysters out of the dressing, mix them with the eggs and pour them in the boiling lard. Don't use more lard than for plain omelet.

MRS. G. E. MILLER.

# MEATS.

### Rules for Boiling Meat.

All fresh meat should be put to cook in boiling water, then the outer part contracts and the internal juices are preserved.

All salt meats should be put on in cold water, that the salt may be extracted in the cooking.

In boiling meats it is important to keep the water constantly boiling, otherwise the meat will absorb the water. be careful to add boiling water if more is needed. Remove the scum when it first begins to boil. The more gently meat boils the more tender it will be. Allow about twenty minutes boiling for each pound of fresh meat.

### Boiled Leg of Mutton.

Put on in boiling water, with a little salt; boil two hours and a half. Make a sauce of melted butter (the size of an egg) mixed well with a tablespoon of flour, stir into a pint of boiling water, with a tablespoon of capers. Garnish with hard boiled eggs sliced, or with sliced lemon and parsley.

### Cooking Cold Meats.

Chop the meat fine, season with salt and pepper, a little onion and tomato catsup. Fill a pan two-thirds full, cover it with potatoes which have been well salted and mashed with milk. Lay bits of butter over the top, and set it in the oven for fifteen or twenty minutes.

### Pickled Brains.

Cleanse them well with *hot* but not *boiling* water; put over the fire in tepid water, with a little salt, and bring to a boil. When well cooked let them cool, and heat some vinegar, adding a small quantity of spice; pour over brains, and let them become cold before using.

Mrs. Rob't Archer.

### Broiled Sweet Breads.

Boil the sweet bread twenty minutes, then split it, season with salt and pepper, rub quickly with butter, and sprinkle with flour. Broil over a *rather* quick fire, turning constantly. Cook about ten minutes, and serve with cream sauce.

### Kidney with Tomato Sauce.

Boil one kidney quite tender, changing the water once, puting salt in the last water. Make a sauce of one large tomato stewed with a tablespoon of butter, salt, pepper, one-half teaspoon of flour, a few sprigs of parsley. After sauce is cooked add kidney sliced.

### Broiled Kidney.

Cut the kidney open, broil, season with salt, pepper, and plenty of butter.

### Chicken and Ham Pie.

Line a dish with paste; season with pepper and salt a few slices of ham and chicken, place them alternately in the dish, covering each layer with the yelks of hard boiled eggs; fill up the dish with gravy, in which half a cup of tomato sauce has been put; cover with paste; cook until well done. If too dry, add gravy when served.

### Croquettes.

Take turkey, chicken, or meat of any kind, with slices of ham, fat and lean, chopped together very fine, add half as much stale bread, grated, also salt, pepper and catsup, grated nutmeg and a lump of butter, knead all together, mold in some flat shape, dip in the yolk of an egg, cover with bread crumbs and fry a light brown. Mrs. Judge Thomson.

### Yacht Pie.

A fellow can always get a live, tough chicken on a cruise. Martha's Vineyard chickens are the toughest. Well, you wash your chicken and cut it all up. Take some of the salt junk that you ought to have on board, and cook it for an hour in fresh water, make a paste of flour and butter—half a pound of butter to a pound of flour. Take an iron pot and rub it all

MEATS.

over with butter; make a piece of the paste round like the top of your hat, and clap it on the bottom of your pot and another long piece to go all around; stow away at the bottom a layer of beef; slice two big onions and three potatoes and put in a few pieces, and pepper that, then put in your chicken and more potato and onion, and ballast the whole thing that way. When you have arrived at the deck of the pot put in a tablespoonful of Worcester sauce and about the same of tomato catsup and three pints of cold water; lash on the cover of the pot, and let her cook gently for four hours. If she burns you are gone. She wants watching. If your junk is salt, you need not add salt; if quite fresh, add some. You catch some fish on next summer's cruise and try this way, using bacon for beef. The more ladies you have on board, the more onions should be used.

### Potted Beef.

Take a beef shin, cover with boiling water, boil until perfectly tender, remove the bone, put the meat back into the liquor, season with salt, pepper and spices that you may fancy, boil down and press into shape; eat cold.

Mrs. Judge Thomson.

### To Smother Fowls.

Dust the fowl with flour; put it in a shallow pan, pour in a tumbler of warm water, and cover with a lid or plate and set the pan in the oven As soon as the fowl is warm, begin to baste with butter, and continue this until it is nearly done; remove the cover, and brown the fowl until done. Cook the giblets in very little water, mince and add to the gravy and pour over the fowl.

Squirrels and the hind legs and loins of rabbits are good served in the same way.

### Croquettes of Poultry.

Take any kind of cold fowl, chop very fine and grind it with a rolling-pin; soak an equal quantity of stale bread, with just enough milk and water to moisten it; press the bread crumbs, adding an equal amount of butter; work into the

MEATS.

mixture the yelks of three hard boiled eggs, grated fine; season with salt and pepper. Beat the whites of two eggs to a stiff froth, stir into the other ingredients. Make this mixture into small cakes and fry in hot lard; take up free of grease, and garnish the dish with celery or lemons cut in thin slices.

### To Broil Quail.

After dressing, split down the back, sprinkle with salt and pepper, and lay them on a gridiron, the inside down. Broil slowly at first. Have ready a hot platter with buttered toast. While broiling, use butter on them, and turn in cooking.

Rabbit broiled in this way is nice.

### A Nice Way to Cook Chicken.

Cut the chicken up, put into a pan, and cover with water; let it stew as usual. When done, make a thickening of melted butter and flour, or of cream and flour, add butter, pepper and salt, have ready a nice short cake, baked and cut in squares, or fresh baked biscuit broken open and put upon a dish and pour the chicken and gravy over them while hot.

### Roast Turkey.

To dress a medium-sized turkey, take one small loaf of bread grated fine, or break the crust and crumb fine with the hand, season with salt, pepper and butter, a little sage if liked. Always put the giblets under the side of the fowl so they will not dry up. Rub pepper and salt on the outside, put into dripping pan with one pint of water, baste often, turn till brown all over, take out the giblets when done, chop fine. After taking out the turkey, add to the gravy a large tablespoon of flour; let it boil up, and then add the giblets.

### Turkey Dressed with Oysters.

For a ten-pound turkey, take two pints of bread crumbs, half a teacup of butter (cut in bits, not melted), pepper, salt, a little parsley, or summer savory, if liked, mix thoroughly. Rub the turkey well, inside and out, with salt and pepper, then fill with first a spoonful of crumbs, then a few well drained oysters, using a pint for a turkey. Strain the oyster

MEATS.

liquor and use to baste the turkey. Cook the giblets and chop fine for the gravy. A fowl of this size will require, for roasting, three hours in a moderate oven.

### Boiled Turkey.

Soak in salt water for an hour and a half to make it white; make the stuffing of bread crumbs and about half the quantity of suet, a little parsley chopped fine. Scald the parsley in order to have it green. Put all this in the breast, tie tightly in a cloth and boil. A young turkey will boil in two hours; an older one will require three or four hours. Garnish with parsley and lemon cut in thin slices.

### Scalloped Ham.

Take pieces of Ham, not fit for slicing, chopped fine; take an equal quantity of crackers, roll and moisten with milk. Into a patty-pan put layer of ham and then of cracker. In centre of each pan make a depression with spoon, into which break one egg (being careful not to break the yelk); season with salt, pepper and butter. Put in the oven, by time egg is cooked the whole will be ready to serve. Send to table in pans.

### Pig's Head.

Have the head nicely cleaned, and boil until very tender; chop very fine, season with salt and pepper while hot, and if agreeable, add sage and cloves. Put into a deep dish and cover with a plate that is smaller than the dish, that it may rest on the meat. Place on the plate a very heavy weight and let it stand for twenty-four hours.

### Ham Croquettes.

One cup of deviled ham, one cup of powdered crackers, mix with two well beaten eggs; dip in beaten egg, then in crumbs, and fry in boiling lard.    Mrs. Judge Thomson.

### Deviled Ham.

Use the remains of cold ham. Take one-third fat and two-thirds lean, cut out all hard, dark bits, chop as fine as possible, and make a dressing as follows: This for three pounds; one tablespoonful of white sugar, one teaspoonful of dry

MEATS.                                               35

mustard, one salt-spoon of cayenne pepper, one cup good vinegar. Mix well with ham, and mould in a bowl.

Mrs. Judge Thomson.

### Hog's Head Cheese.

Take a hog's head, have it nicely cleaned, cover with water, boil until very tender. Chop very fine, add salt, pepper, cloves and allspice; pour the liquor it was boiled in over it, return to the fire; stir frequently until it thickens; skim off the fat that rises to the top. When very thick pour in molds; let it stand all night, then turn it out bottom upwards. If well done it will be a beautiful jelly.     Mrs. J. R. Hutchison.

### Boiled Ham.

Put the ham to soak in cold water the evening before boiling it. The next morning take it out and put it in a pot of fresh water on the stove. Let it boil two hours, then change the water, being careful to have boiling water to replace the water throw out. Continue to boil the ham until well done. Take it off the fire, throw the water off again and put it in a pan of cold water.

### Baked Ham.

Take a medium-sized ham, wash and scrape well, cover it with water and soak over night; make a dough of flour and water, roll it out and cover the ham with it completely. Put it in a baking pan and bake about four hours, and baste frequently with boiling water to prevent the dough cracking off. When done, take from the oven and let it become cold, then remove all the dough and trim the ham as if it were boiled.

Mrs. T. J. Girardeau.

### Melton Veal.

Veal may be cooked in dozens of ways. It is not as nutritious as beef or mutton, but in many places is much cheaper. Cooked with ham or bacon, it has a fine flavor. One method of cooking the two together is to line a large bowl, which is well buttered, with slices of hard boiled eggs, then alternate thin slices of veal and ham, sprinkling pepper, salt and grated lemon rind on the veal, pepper and lemon on

## MEATS.

the ham. Fill the bowl nearly to the brim, make a thick paste of flour and water, cover over the top and press tight to the outside edges of the bowl. Put into water (not enough to boil over the paste) and boil three hours. Leave the paste on until nearly cold; do not turn out of the bowl until next morning; then, if the bowl was well buttered, you find a very appetizing-looking dish. Cut in very thin slices, it is excellent as a supper, breakfast or side dish at dinner.

### Economical French Dish.

Few of us care for cold meat any length of time, but we can make a delicious dish out of slices of cold beef or mutton. Take a deep baking dish, slice your meat thin and cut off the grizzled edges, put a layer in the dish, dust over pepper, salt and sifted sweet marjoram or sage, or, if liked, a chopped onion. Fill your dish half full in this manner, then add the cold gravy left from the roast, taking off every particle of fat; turn in half a teacup of catsup or a quantity of canned or fresh, ripe tomatoes. Fill the dish nearly full with boiling water and put a plate over it, right side down; this keeps all the flavor in the dish. Bake two hours in the oven; wash some potatoes with butter, or cream and salt, make with it a high wall around the edge of a heated platter, beat up an egg, and brush over the wall and brown in oven, then turn the meat and gravy inside the platter and serve.

### Potted Meat.

Boil the knee and shank of beef till perfectly tender. If there is no lean meat on the shank add two pounds lean veal; all must be boiled together. When done remove the meat from the water and mince it very fine; season to taste with salt, pepper and spice; return to the water and boil again, stirring all the time; boil until it will jelly; put into molds and allow it to cool. A pig's foot boiled with it is an improvement.

### A Nice Way to Prepare Beefsteak.

Take a large beefsteak, scatter over it pieces of butter, salt and pepper, and a little sage and finely chopped onions, over that spread a thick cushion of mashed potatoes, well seasoned with salt, fresh butter, and a very little milk; roll up the steak with the potatoes inside, fasten the side and ends with skewers; put the steak in a baking pan with a cupful of stock; let it cook slowly, basting like chicken. Serve with a rim of mashed potatoes around it, and garnished with parsley.

Mrs. C. S. House.

### A Nice Way to Prepare Steak.

Pound the steak well, have ready a very hot, dry frying pan, put in the steak and cover tight, have ready in a meat dish butter, pepper and salt. As the juice cooks from the steak, pour it into the dish, turn and brown on the other side. When done, saturate well in the gravy and serve hot.

### Beefsteak Smothered with Onions.

Put into the skillet a little lard; when hot, lay in the steak, cover it with sliced onions, well seasoned with salt and pepper; cover tightly. After the juices of the onion are boiled away and the meat begins to fry, remove the onions and turn the meat to brown on the other side, then replace the onions, being careful that they do not burn.

### Nice Way to Cook a Round of Beef.

Make incisions through and through the beef with a sharp knife, and fill them with the following mixture: Cut three or four onions very fine, with several slices of ham, both lean and fat; mix with this three teaspoons of dry mustard, salt to taste, not quite a teaspoon each of allspice and mace. Tie the round firmly with a string, making the incisions close as much as possible. Cover the whole entirely with vinegar, sprinkled slightly with salt; let it stand awhile. Bake slowly, without water or any of the vinegar, and you will have a rich gravy.

Mrs. Judge Thomson, Virginia.

### Beef a la Mode.

Take five pounds of the round of beef, four or five inches thick, and with a steel make holes entirely through it at small distances apart, then take strips of fat salt pork, roll them in pepper, cloves and allspice, and put them into the holes in the beef. Put it into a steamer and steam three hours. When done, thicken the gravy in a pan with flour. This is also very nice when eaten cold without the gravy.

### Veal Collops.

Cut veal from the leg or other lean parts into pieces the size of an oyster. Have a seasoning of pepper, salt and mace mixed. Rub some over each piece, then dip in egg, roll in cracker crumbs and fry as you do oysters. They both look and taste like oysters.

### Spiced Beef.

Get a round of beef weighing ten pounds, tie it close together in good shape (round) with tape, take one tablespoon ground mace, one of cloves, one of allspice, and one of saltpeter, and rub the meat well with the spices mixed. Place the meat in a deep dish, set aside, and turn over every morning for ten mornings. When ready for cooking, place it in a pot, with the spices, liquor and all. Cover with water and cook four hours. To be eaten cold for luncheon or tea.

### Broiled Venison Steak.

Cut thick, pound well, season with pepper and salt, broil quickly over a clear fire. Eat while hot, on hot plates.

### Veal Croquettes.

Prepare the cold veal as for hash, then press with the hands into small, flat cakes; flour well, and fry in hot lard till brown.

### Stuffed Veal.

Take the hind quarter of veal, three slices of pork, three slices of bread, three eggs, salt and pepper. Chop the meat and bread to a fine hash, add the beaten eggs, and soak it all in milk. Fill the cavity made by taking the bone from the veal; rub lard over it; bake two hours. Good hot or cold.

### Veal Loaf.

Three and a half pounds of veal, lean and fat, chopped fine, one slice of salt pork, six small crackers, rolled fine, butter size of an egg, two eggs, one tablespoon of salt, pepper and sage, three tablespoons of celery. Mix thoroughly, pack tightly in a deep, square tin, cover with bits of butter and sprinkle cracker crumbs over the top; cover with another tin; bake two hours, uncover and brown the top.

AGNES L. DWIGHT, Chicago, Ill.

### Veal Cutlets with Oysters.

Take a pint of oysters with their liquor, grate a tumbler almost full of cracker crumbs, add to the oysters, season with pepper and sauce. Prepare half a dozen cutlets. Put a pint of lard into a frying pan, when boiling hot, roll the cutlets in flour and drop them in the hot lard, watching carefully to keep them from scorching. When half done, pour off the lard and add the oysters. Take up when the oysters begin to shrink. Serve in a covered dish. If the gravy is not thick enough, add a little flour.

### Breaded Veal.

Take veal chops, cutlets or steak, have ready bread crumbs, grated fine, dip the meat first into beaten egg and then into the bread crumbs, and fry brown in very hot lard.

### Veal Stuffed with Oysters.

Take a fillet of veal, prepare for roasting, make a rich dressing, using as many oysters as you do bread crumbs. Make incisions with a sharp knife all over your piece of veal, press into them whole oysters, together with some of the dressing. Spread the dressing over the top of the meat and roast. A few whole oysters added to the gravy improves the flavor very much.  MRS. T. C. ARMSTRONG.

### Calf's Head—No. 1.

Thoroughly cleanse a nice calf's head, and boil in water until you can easily remove bones; chop fine and add allspice, black pepper, red pepper, and nutmeg, catsup, currant or blackberry jelly, one cup wine, celery seed, mustard, salt, butter and herbs—all these to your taste. Serve in a tureen. Cut hard boiled eggs and place over the top. Forced meat balls, fried and brown fritters laid on top to garnish the dish.

### Calf's Head—No. 2.

Have the head nicely cleaned, and boil until very tender, so that you can put a straw through it. When boiled sufficiently, take out the bones, season with salt and pepper, and a little vinegar. Put in a dish, press by putting a plate on, and a heavy weight on plate. It is nice sliced cold or warmed in drawn butter, or if you prefer, and wish to use soon after being cooked, you can leave out the vinegar.

### Sweet Breads Broiled.

Par-boil after soaking in salt water, then rub well with butter and broil. Turn often, and dip into melted butter to prevent their getting hard and dry.

### Sweet Breads Fried.

Wash in salt and water, par-boil, cut into pieces the size of a large oyster; season with salt and pepper; roll in fine cracker crumbs, and fry a light brown in lard and butter.

### Wine Stew.

To one large vegetable dish of cold mutton, or beef sliced, add one tablespoon of damson preserves (any other preserves can be substituted), one teacup tomato catsup, one teacup butter, one-half nutmeg grated, two teacups of wine, four tablespoons of currant jelly. Add the last two ingredients a very short time before taking off the fire; use salt, pepper and mustard to your taste; add water enough to make a nice stew. If desirable, a small piece of onion improves the flavor. Stew slowly until done.

### A Good Stuffing for Turkey, Fowls, Etc.

Cut bread in thin slices and toast, break and roll it fine and mix with enough water to make a paste. Take the gizzard and liver and cut very fine, three large onions cut very fine, put a large tablespoonful of lard in a frying pan. When hot, add the liver and gizzard and let fry a few minutes, then the onions, then the bread; salt, pepper and let cook for a quarter of an hour. If too dry, moisten with a little hot water. Sausage meat with the other meat and onions, before adding the bread, is very nice, or oysters added after the stuffing is cooked.

# SAUCES FOR MEATS.

### Sauce for Fish.

The yelks of three eggs, one tablespoon sugar, half pound of butter and salt to taste. Place on fire until it thickens. It must only get warm, as it will curdle or spoil.

Mrs. Jane Connell.

### Dressing for Crabs or Boiled Fish.

A tablespoon of butter, creamed with mustard, salt, pepper, vinegar, and the yelks of two raw eggs. Mix well, then put on fire and stir until it becomes the consistency of custard.

### Drop Dumplings for Meat.

Scald a pint of milk or water. Make a paste by stirring sufficient cold milk in a tumblerful of sifted flour. When the pint of milk boils pour into the paste, stirring constantly until bubbles begin to form on the top. Pour it into a bowl, and let it remain until cold. Beat two eggs well, then beat them with the batter, and add more flour until a stiff batter is made; salt to taste; drop by spoonfuls in the stew. Eight or ten minutes will cook them sufficiently. Mace is sometimes used for seasoning stews.

### Caper Sauce.

Melt a quarter of a pound of butter, into which two teaspoonfuls of flour has been rubbed, add two tumblers of sweet milk, or one of milk and one of water, and six or eight tablespoonfuls of capers.

Mock caper sauce may be made by using pickles cut up small in place of capers.

### Drawn Butter Sauce.

Put two-thirds of a pint of water in a sauce-pan and set it on the fire to boil, make a paste of three teaspoonfuls of flour with a little water. When the water in the sauce-pan boils, add the flour, stirring well. Let it boil a few minutes, then add a heaping tablespoonful of butter.

Mrs. G. A. McDonell.

### Dressing for Salads, Meats, Salmon, Etc.

Six eggs well beaten, six tablespoonfuls melted butter, six tablespoonfuls cream, two tablespoonfuls mustard, two tablespoonfuls black pepper, one tablespoon salt, two coffee-cups of vinegar. Boil all the ingredients except the eggs; when thoroughly mixed, pour it over the eggs, stirring all the while, then set it over the fire until it simmers; remove quickly to prevent its being too thick. Mrs. B. D. Orgain.

### Cream Sauce.

One pint of cream, one heaping tablespoon of flour, salt and pepper to taste. Let the cream come to a boil. Have the flour mixed smooth, with one-half cup of cream reserved from the pint, and stir it into the boiling cream. Add seasoning and boil three minutes. This sauce is good for delicate meats, fish and vegetables, and to pour around croquettes and baked omelettes.

### A Good Mayonnaisse Dressing.

Put the yelks of two eggs in a deep dish, with a little salt and white pepper; into these stir briskly some olive oil; add a few spoonfuls of vinegar. This dressing should have an agreeable flavor, and a rather stiff consistency. Salad oil should be kept well corked in a dry, cool place, and always in the dark.

### Apple Vinegar.

To two bushels of apples well beaten, add ten gallons of water. Let this stand until well fermented, then draw it off and put in jugs; tie a cloth over the mouth of each jug and let it stand until it is good vinegar, then cork tightly.

### Vinegar.

Seven and a half gallons hot water, three quarts molasses, three quarts whisky, three-fourths of a pint of yeast. Put this mixture in a ten-gallon cask with a piece of brown paper,

SAUCES FOR MEATS.

Nail a double piece of osnaberg over the bung, and set the cask in the sun to remain six weeks.

### Pickle for Tongues or Ham.

One gallon of clear water, one and one-half pounds salt, one pound brown sugar, one ounce saltpetre, one ounce allspice. Scald and skim, and let it become cold before putting in the tongues. MRS. T. C. ARMSTRONG.

### Mustard Sauce.

Mix into a paste, four tablespoons of mustard, the yelks of four eggs, one cup of good vinegar, three tablespoons of brown sugar, one cup of butter, about three teaspoons of cayenne pepper, salt to taste. Cook, and stir constantly to prevent scorching, until it thickens. It will keep a year, and is nice in any kind salad dressing.

### Worcestershire Sauce.

Take one gallon of ripe tomatoes, wash, and simmer them in three quarts of water; boil it half down and strain through a seive. When all is drained, add two tablespoonfuls of ginger, two of mace, two of whole black pepper, two of salt, one of cloves, one of cayenne. Let them simmer in the juice until reduced to one quart; pour in half pint of best vinegar, then pour the whole through a hair sieve. Bottle in half-pint bottles, cork down, tightly seal, and keep in a cool place.

### Celery Sauce.

Boil the white parts of several stalks of celery, cutting them in small pieces, in two tumblerfuls of boiling water. Add salt to taste, and cover the stew-pan; let simmer until tender. Rub heaped teaspoonful of flour into a piece of butter the size of an egg, strain the water from the celery on this, remove the celery from the pan, wipe out the pan, return the broth to it, and add a tumbler of sweet cream, or fresh milk, let this simmer a short time and it is ready to serve. Particularly nice for wild duck roasted. MRS. C. S. HOUSE.

### Parsley Sauce.

Boil several sprigs of parsley in a tumbler of water about ten minutes, pick off the leaves, chop fine and salt to taste.

Wipe out the stew pan, return the water and add to it an equal quantity of sweet milk. Make a paste of a teaspoonful of flour and little cold milk. When the milk and water boils, stir in the paste, add a tumbler of fresh butter, then stir in gradually the minced parsley. Lemon juice may be added, and it is nice for broiled or boiled fish.

Mrs C. S. House.

### Common Mustard.

One tablespoonful of ground mustard, one teaspoonful of sugar, one saltspoonful of salt. Mix all together, and then pour on boiling water, stirring it well until quite smooth, make as thick as you like.     Mrs. N. A. Milton.

# HASH.

### Ham Hash.

Take double the quantity of potatoes that you have of ham; chop up the ham, and after boiling the potatoes, mash them up and mix with the ham. Season with salt, pepper, butter and one beaten egg. Put all in a pan and bake brown.

Mrs. A. J. Burke.

### Hash.

Chop the meat very fine, with cold Irish potatoes; season with onion, pepper and salt; place in a sauce-pan, with very little water, and slowly simmer for a short time.

### Baked Hash.

Prepare as above, and put in baking dish, with a little water put over the meat, some small pieces of butter, and then cover the whole with bread crumbs, grated fine. Bake till brown. Some persons prefer to soak the bread crumbs in a cup of milk, with an egg beaten in before using them.

### Fried Hash.

Prepare the meat as for hash, then flour it well; have ready a frying pan, with a little very hot lard in it, pour the hash in, stirring often, and cook dry and brown.

### Pigshead Hash.

Boil the head, with little salt, until very tender, then chop the meat as other hash; season with pepper, onions, parsley—sage, if you like; return to the fire until the ingredients are well cooked.

Mrs. Robt. Archer.

### Fish Hash.

Take any kind of cooked fish, mince the meat fine and season with pepper, have a third as much Irish potatoes, mashed fine, as there is fish. Cut up three hard boiled eggs, stir this mixture together, add a tumbler of boiling water and large spoonful of butter. Stir the fish into the stew-pan and simmer until hot. Serve at once in a hot dish.

# CATSUP.

### Tomato Catsup—No. 1.

One-half bushel of tomatoes, one quart of vinegar, one pound of salt, one-fourth pound of black pepper in the grain, one-half ounce of capsicum, or one ounce very hot, one-fourth pound of allspice in grain, one ounce of cloves, one-fourth pound of mustard, three pounds of brown sugar, six onions, and one handful of peach leaves. Boil all together for three hours. When sufficiently cool, rub through coarse sieve, and bottle. This catsup does not mold.

Mrs. James Bailey.

### Pepper Catsup.

Boil four dozen ripe or green hot peppers in two quarts of vinegar until soft enough to mash through a sieve, leaving nothing but the skins to throw away; add salt to the taste, two tablespoons of black pepper, one of allspice, one-third of cloves, three of horseradish, five onions. Boil the whole ten minutes. If thicker than you like, thin it with vinegar. Be careful not to let it get on the hands.

Mrs. Rob't Archer.

### Green Tomato Sauce.

Two gallons green tomatoes, three tablespoons of mustard, three gills of mustard seed, one and one-half tablespoons of pepper, one of allspice, three of salt, one of cloves, one pint chopped onions, one quart of sugar, five pints of vinegar. Boil well.

### Tomato Catsup—No. 2.

To one gallon ripe tomatoes, cut up, put four tablespoons of salt, four of ground pepper, three tablespoons of allspice, the same of cloves, ground fine, six pods of pepper, broken up.

Simmer the whole slowly three or four hours. A short time before taking from the fire, add one pint of vinegar, and one pint of chopped onions may be added to the catsup if preferred—add before cooking. When cold, put in strong bottles. Place the bottles in warm water, heating them thoroughly to expel the air; seal tightly, and it will keep for years. Use a porcelain kettle for cooking.

### Tomato Soy.

Seven pounds ripe tomatoes, three and one-half pounds sugar, one quart vinegar, and spices to taste. Boil until like marmalade.

### Tomato Catsup—No 3.

Can be made of fresh or canned tomatoes. Take one can, strain through a colander; add salt, pepper, cloves, allspice, cinnamon and vinegar to taste, boil until thick.

Mrs. J. R. Hutchison.

### Tomato Catsup—No. 4.

One peck tomatoes, one-half ounce black pepper, one-half ounce cloves, three ounces mustard seed, one garlic root. Boil the tomatoes and stain through a sieve; add to this the other ingredients, and salt to taste. Boil until reduced one-half, then add one tablespoonful of mustard to every quart of the spiced tomatoes.  Mrs. E. D. Junkin.

### Tomato Catsup—No. 5

Cut up the tomatoes; boil over a slow fire until all the juice may be extracted; strain through a sieve, and let it boil fast, stirring it frequently; then to each gallon of juice, add the following: One quart of vinegar, four tablespoons of salt, four tablespoons of ground black pepper, three tablespoons of mustard, two of mixed spices, eight pods of red pepper, two large onions, chopped fine. Boil until thick.

Mrs. Wm. Christian.

### Green Tomato Soy.

Two gallons tomatoes, green, and sliced without peeling, twelve good sized onions also sliced, two quarts vinegar, one quart sugar, two table spoons salt, two tablespoons ground mustard, two tablespoons black pepper, ground, one tablespoon allspice, one tablespoon cloves. Mix all together, and stew until tender, stirring often to prevent scorching. Put up in small glass jars. Mrs. J. L. Cunningham.

### Cucumber Catsup.

Twelve large cucumbers, four onions, one-half teacupful of mustard seed, one tablespoonful of black pepper. Peel and chop fine the cucumbers, also the onions. Spread a thick layer of the onions and cucumbers in a dish, alternating with very thin layers of salt. Cover and let stand one night; next morning press out through a bag all the water that can be pressed out of this mixture. If it is too salt, put fresh water over it for an hour or two, then press again until dry. Mix with it then the mustard and pepper; cover with vinegar and put up in bottles, corking tightly. Even after being kept some time this will taste like fresh cucumbers.

Mrs. E. D. Junkin.

### Cucumber Catsup.

Pare and grate six cucumbers, mix with two onions, chopped fine, add vinegar, pepper, salt and spices to taste. Put up and cork tightly. In a few days it will be ready for use.

Mrs. J. R. Hutchison.

# PICKLES

### Chow-Chow—No. 1.

One head cabbage, chopped fine, six cucumbers, six onions, one pint green tomatoes, one pint snap beans, chopped fine, two tablespoons salt and pepper (black and red) to suit taste. Cover with vinegar; let it boil down to about half. When taken off fire, add two teaspoons sweet oil.

Mrs. J. R. Hutchison

### Higden Salad.

Take equal quantities of cabbage, green tomatoes and about half as much of onions and green bell-peppers, chop them fine together and put them in a jar; salt to taste, and let them remain in brine a few hours. Drain and let it lie in plain vinegar twenty-four hours. Squeeze out the vinegar and season with mustard seed, horseradish and black pepper, etc. Put the pickles back in the jar and fill up with strong vinegar. It will be fit for use in a week. Mrs. G. A. McDonell.

### Mangoes—To Prepare for Stuffing.

Take melons a little larger than a goose egg, pour strong salt boiling water over them and cover up. Next day cut a slit in the side of each melon, take out the inside and return the rinds to the brine. Let them remain eight days, then put them in strong vinegar for two weeks. Wipe the inside of each mango with a soft cloth, stuff and tie. Pack with the slit uppermost.

### Stuffing for Mangoes.

For a three gallon jar, one cup black pepper (not ground), one ounce allspice, one-half ounce ginger, one-half ounce mace, one-half ounce cloves, one cup celery seed, two cups grated horseradish, one quart mustard seed, five pounds brown sugar.

Beat the spices, but not too fine. Mix half the spices thus beaten with the horseradish and mustard seed. Rub the inside of each mango with a teaspoonful of sugar and fill with the mixture. Pack closely in a jar and cover with vinegar, mixed with the rest of the sugar and spices.

Mrs. E. E. Junkin.

### Pepper Mangoes.

Take the cap out of the pod, then scrape out the seed, lay the pods in salt water for one hour. Chop cabbage very fine and to every quart, add one tablespoonful of salt, one tablespoonful of ground black pepper, two tablespoons of white mustard seed, one tablespoonful of cloves, one of cinnamon one cup of sugar. Mix all together. Drain the pepper pods and stuff them with the mixture, replace the cap, pack them closely in a stone jar, then pour on them strong vinegar. They are ready for use in a few weeks.

### Peach Mangoes.

Take large peaches, peel nicely and take out the stones. Have ready the stuffing in proportion to the peaches. Chop up some of the peaches, add a large quantity of mustard seed, a good deal of sugar, ground ginger, cinnamon, cloves, pepper, turmeric and celery seed. Stuff the peaches and sew them up. To every pound of sugar, add one-half pint of vinegar, allowing this quantity to every two pounds of fruit. Make a syrup of the sugar and vinegar, and pour over the stuffed peaches.

Mrs. J. A. Peebles.

### Chili Sauce—No. 1.

Twenty-four large ripe tomatoes, eight green peppers, eight onions, three tablespoonfuls salt, three tablespoons cinnamon, three of cloves, three of ginger, eight tablespoons of sugar. Scald and peel the tomatoes and cook well, chop onions and peppers fine, then mix all ingredients and cook until thick and brown; bottle tight.

Mrs. T. W. House.

### Cucumber Pickles.

Lay cucumbers in brine; be sure to make your brine strong enough to bear an egg, and boil the brine before using. When

PICKLES.

ready to pickle the cucumbers, if they are too salt, freshen. Place them in a kettle, with small piece of alum, and cabbage leaves at top and bottom. Cover with water and scald until green. Wipe them dry and place in a jar. Boil the vinegar with spice, black and red pepper and onions. Pour while hot over the cucumbers. When cold, add two tablespoons of mustard.

### Pickles.

Fill a gallon jar about three-fourths full of small ladyfinger peppers, cover with best white wine vinegar in which one-half pound salt has been dissolved, seal tight and set aside for four weeks, when they will be ready for use.

### Chow-Chow—No. 2.

One gallon chopped cabbage, one-half gallon green tomatoes, one quart onions, six pods green peppers from which seed have been extracted, all chopped fine and mixed. Let stand all night, then strain off liquor and throw away. Put pickle in kettle, together with one tablespoon ground mustard, two ounces ginger, two ounces cinnamon, three ounces cloves and three of salt, one ounce of celery seed, one gallon vinegar. Boil all together until vegetables are tender and clear. When this is the case, put in jars and seal while hot.      A. W.

### Chili Sauce—No. 2.

Twelve large tomatoes, three large green peppers, one-half cup sugar, one tablespoon salt, one-half tablespoon black pepper, three large onions one teacup of vinegar. Chop all fine and cook over a slow fire three hours.      A. W.

### Yellow Pickles.

Two and one-half gallons of very best vinegar, seven pounds brown sugar, one pound white mustard, one bottle mustard, one pound white ginger, one-half pound of turmeric, two ounces nutmeg, two ounces mace, two ounces allspice, two ounces cloves, two ounces celery seed, one pound scraped horseradish, one-half dozen lemons, two dozen onions. Pound all the seed and spices, put them in the vinegar, then add the horseradish and sliced lemons. Scald the onions, sprinkle them with salt, and let them stand for a day, then drain off the water, and wash them in vinegar, then drain again carefully and add to the spiced vinegar. Scald the cabbage in salt and water until you can pierce with a straw, drain it for a day, and put it in plain vinegar for two weeks, then let it drain a day before putting it to the spiced vinegar.

### Chili Sauce—No. 3.

Eighteen ripe tomatoes, pared, three green peppers, one onion, one cup sugar, two and one-half cups vinegar, two teaspoons salt, one teaspoon cinnamon, one of cloves. Cook the tomatoes until tender; chop the onion and peppers fine. Mix all and cook a few minutes. A few leaves of mint added to pickles are an improvement.

### Green Tomato Pickles.

Chop very fine half peck green tomatoes, and sprinkle with salt. Let them remain twelve hours, then drain the water from them and add onions, horseradish, dozen green peppers, quarter pound of white mustard seed, a few pieces of ginger, and one teaspoon of ground black pepper. Put mixture in a close vessel and cover with boiling vinegar. When cold it is ready for use. Mrs. McDonell.

### Spiced Tomatoes.

Pulp one pound of tomatoes; add one pound sugar. After boiling slowly for two hours add one large glass of vinegar, one tablespoonful of cloves and allspice. Boil one hour.

Mrs. Adey.

# SWEET PICKLES.

### Tomato Sweet Pickle—No. 1.

Seven pounds ripe tomatoes, peeled and sliced, three and one-half pounds sugar, one quart vinegar, cloves and spice to taste. Mix all together and cook one hour.

Mrs. Rob't Wilson.

### Cucumber Sweet Pickle.

One gallon of pickles, sliced thin, one quart vinegar, three pints white sugar, mace, ginger and cloves, lemons cut up in it. Let syrup boil well before putting in the cucumbers. When the cucumbers are put in, let it come to a boil, and take them out. Mrs. Jno. D. Rogers, Galveston.

### Green Tomato Sweet Pickle.

One peck of green tomatoes, slice them in the afternoon, six onions, sliced in the same way; sprinkle salt between layers of each, and let remain over night, then drain carefully. Put all on the fire in a kettle of fresh water and boil until thoroughly done, then drain over a colander, and lay out on dishes to cool. One gallon best vinegar, three pounds sugar one-half ounce mace, one box mustard, one-half ounce ginger, one teacup oil, one-half ounce cloves, one tablespoon black pepper, ground. Mix all, and put in the fruit cold.

### Watermelon Sweet Pickle.

Prepare your rind as for preserve. Let it remain over night in lime water. In the morning wash carefully and put in clear water, adding a piece of alum about the size of a walnut, pounded finely; let them come to a boil, then to seven pounds of rind make a syrup of three pounds of sugar and one quart vinegar. To clarify the syrup, crush an egg with the vinegar; while boiling, skim carefully and strain. When the syrup is ready, add the rind and juice of a lemon, also cinnamon, spice, mace, ginger root and cloves to suit the taste. Let it boil for two or three hours, being careful to remove all the scum that may rise. If the syrup should boil too thick add a little more vinegar. MRS. C. E. ATKINSON...

### Peach Sweet Pickle—No. 1.

Seven pounds peaches, three pounds good brown sugar, one quart vinegar, one teaspoon cinnamon, one of cloves, one of spice. Boil the sugar, vinegar and spices fifteen minutes, then add peaches and boil until tender. MRS MILTON.

### Peach Sweet Pickle—No. 2.

Put your peaches in brine and let them remain two or three days. Take them out and wash and wipe them dry, stick three or four cloves in each and put in a jar. To each quart of vinegar allow one pound of sugar and some allspice and pepper. Let it come to a boil and pour it over the peaches.

### Plum Sweet Pickle.

Three pounds of fruit, one pound sugar, one quart vinegar, and spices to the taste. Boil sugar and vinegar together and then put in fruit, and boil until thick enough to keep.

### Tomato Sweet Pickle—No. 2.

Slice small tomatoes; put alternate layers of tomatoes and brown sugar in stone jars. When full put saucer on top and let stand in a cool place. In a short time it will make its own vinegar. Add spices.

### Sweet Pickle.

One pound of sugar to one pint vinegar, spices, cloves, cinnamon, mace to taste. Put in as much fruit as syrup will cover well, and boil from fifteen to thirty minutes.

MRS. I. D. SAYERS, Bastrop.

### Pickled Peaches—No. 4.

Three teaspoonfuls powdered cloves, one quart strong cider vinegar. Let vinegar, sugar and spices boil, then put in peaches and boil until a straw can be stuck through them with ease. Take out and put in earthen jars; pour over them the vinegar, cover lightly and set away. Next day pour off vinegar and heat until boiling hot and pour over fruit. Repeat this three days, scalding four times, then tie up and set away.

Mrs. J. L. Cunningham.

### Peach Sweet Pickle—No. 3.

Peel peaches; to three pounds peaches add two pounds sugar, one pint vinegar, spice, cloves, cinnamon, black pepper to suit taste. Boil together until done. Mrs. Haynie.

### Pickled Peaches—No. 5.

Ten pounds fruit pared, four and a half pounds sugar, one quart vinegar, spices, *ad libitum.* Lay the peaches in the sugar for an hour, drain off every drop of juice and put over the fire, with a cup of water. Boil until the scum ceases to rise and skim well. Put in fruit and boil five minutes; take out fruit with a skimmer and spread out to cool. Add the vinegar and spices to the syrup. Boil fifteen minutes longer and pour over the fruit in glass jars. B. W.

### Green Tomato Pickles.

Slice one peck green tomatoes, six green bell-peppers, six onions. Sprinkle all with one cup of salt. Let it stand over night; in the morning drain. Take four pints vinegar, one cup grated horseradish, two cups sugar, one tablespoon each of allspice, cloves, cinnamon and black pepper. Put vinegar, etc., on stove, and when boiling pour in tomatoes, pepper and onions. Boil five minutes, or until the peeling wrinkles. Put away in air-tight jars or bottles. Mrs. L. C. Noble.

# SALAD AND SLAW.

### Potato Salad—No. 1.
Boil the potatoes, cut them very fine, add an onion. Make a sauce with a hard boiled egg, pepper, salt, mustard and vinegar. Slice an egg for the top. Mrs. J. R. Hutchison.

### Potato Salad—No. 2.
Cut up very fine some cold Irish potatoes, also one medium sized onion. Boil two or three eggs hard, and cut them up. Mix all together; pour a little melted butter over the whole; season to taste with mustard, pepper and salt. Pour over it enough good vinegar to saturate the whole.

Mrs. E. H. Vincent.

### Potato Salad—No. 3.
Eight medium sized boiled potatoes finely chopped, one small onion chopped *very* fine, two large spoons of finely chopped ham, the same of pickles. Mix thoroughly, and salt to taste.

For dressing, take one small spoon of mustard, also one of black pepper; rub these together with one large spoon of butter; beat one egg and add one teacup of vinegar. Place over the fire and boil a few minutes, until it thickens; pour over the potatoes, and mix. Dress with hard boiled eggs grated over the top.

### Chicken Salad—No. 1.
For a pound of chicken, after it is minced, use six eggs—boil hard—take out the yelks. mash to a smooth paste with a wooden spoon, add half a tumbler of good sweet oil (or melted butter), half a tumbler of good vinegar, two even tablespoons of dry mustard, a tablespoonful of white sugar (dissolved in the vinegar), a teaspoon each of pepper and salt.

Wet the mustard to a paste with the vinegar; mix all these together, mince a third as much celery, mix thoroughly with the fowl, tossing together with a wooden fork. Add the sauce just before serving. Garnish the dish with parsley and the whites of the eggs cut in rings.

### Lobster Salad.

Take a can of lobster—use lettuce instead of celery—make a dressing as for chicken salad and pour over the lobster.

Mrs. T. C. Armstrong, Galveston.

### Cabbage Salad.

Shred the cabbage fine. Heat together two tablespoonfuls of vinegar, one of butter, and a teaspoonful each of salt and sugar. Pour it over the cabbage hot; sprinkle pepper on top and serve.

Mrs. E. C. Blake.

### Chicken Salad—No. 2.

Three chickens boiled; remove the bones and chop fine; juice of two lemons, ten hard boiled eggs, the whites chopped fine; mash the yelks, moisten with six teaspoons melted butter and two of sweet oil, to which add one tablespoon of mustard, one of salt, one of pepper, one of sugar and three of cream; last add six large bunches of celery, chopped fine. Mix all together, with sufficient vinegar to wet the whole.

Miss Agnes L. Dwight.

### Chicken Salad—No. 3.

Two chickens, six hard-boiled eggs, one-half pint vinegar, one-half pound melted butter, two bunches celery, one-half teaspoon cayenne pepper, salt and black pepper to the taste. Boil the fowls, remove all the meat from the bones and take out the skin of the chicken. Chop the meat and celery very fine and mix. Mash the yelks of the eggs, add mustard, butter, pepper, salt and vinegar. Pour the dressing over the meat and mix well together. Mrs. G. A. McDonell.

### Chicken Salad—No. 4.

One fine fat chicken, boiled and boned, same quantity of white cabbage or kraut, six hard boiled eggs, one cup of butter, one pint bottle of pickles, one tablespoonful of mustard, one teaspoonful of salt, one teaspoonful of black pepper, one gill of oil or another half cup of butter. Chop fine the chicken, cabbage, whites of eggs and pickles, and mix them well. Mash the yelks of eggs, add the butter (melted), mustard, stirred in vinegar, salt and pepper, then mix the whole, and, if necessary, add more vinegar till quite soft.

Mrs. B. D. Orgain.

### Chicken Salad—No. 5.

Two cold boiled fowls, yelks of nine hard boiled eggs, one-half pint sweet oil, one-half pint vinegar, four teaspoons of mustard, one of pepper, one of salt, three heads of celery. Chop the celery and chicken very fine. Prepare the dressing, and mix with the chicken and celery. Let the salad stand about an hour before serving.    Mrs. T. C. Armstrong.

### Egg Salad.

Have hard boiled any number of eggs; cut them in halves neatly, remove the yelks, mash smooth, and mix with them salt, pepper, mustard, butter sugar and vinegar to taste; then fill the white halves with this mixture, smoothly rounding it over.    Miss Forman, Cynthiana, Ky.

### Hot Slaw.

Two teaspoons of sugar, one of salt, one cup of vinegar, one spoon of mustard. Mix well together. Chop a cabbage very fine and put in a pan with a tablespoon of water. Get it well heated through. Pour dressing over, place it over the fire until thoroughly heated; take off and serve hot.

Mrs. T. C. Armstrong, Galveston.

### Chicken Salad.

Cut the white meat of chickens into small bits the size of peas, not too fine; chop three-quarters of the same bulk of celery nearly as fine, mix these and set aside in a cold place, while you prepare the dressing. For one chicken or turkey, use the proportions thus: Two hard-boiled eggs, one raw egg well beaten, one teaspoon each of salt, pepper and mustard, three teaspoons salad oil, two teaspoons white sugar, one-half teacup sugar. Rub the yelks to a fine powder, add the salt, pepper and sugar and oil, beating all together, then add the mustard, and the raw egg, whipped to a froth; lastly, the vinegar, pouring in a little at a time, beating all the while. Sprinkle a little salt over the meat and celery, and pour over the dressing, mixing all very carefully. Garnish with white of eggs boiled hard and sprigs of bleached celery tops. You can use crisp, white cabbage as a substitute for celery, and use celery seed or celery vinegar in the dressing.

### Cold Slaw—No. 1.

Have your cabbage finely shred and place in a salad-dish. Put in a sauce-pan one pint vinegar, salt, pepper and sugar to taste, with one tablespoon butter; set over the fire; break in two or three eggs, and stir constantly until it thickens; then add two tablespoons cream. Pour while hot over the cabbage; then cut two or three hard boiled eggs over the top.

Mrs. J. D. Sayers, Bastrop.

### Cold Slaw—No. 2.

Two-thirds of a cup of vinegar, one egg, two tablespoons of sugar, one tablespoon of salt, one-half tablespoon of mixed mustard, butter the size of an egg. Stir until it boils; when cold pour over the shaved cabbage.

### Cold Slaw.

One head white cabbage minced fine, two eggs, two tablespoons salad oil, one tablespoon white sugar, one teaspoon salt, one teaspoon pepper, one teaspoon made mustard, one teaspoon mustard seed, one teacup vinegar. Mix vinegar, mustard, pepper, salt and sugar, put them over the fire to boil; if the vinegar is very strong, add a little water. Beat one egg very light and mix with it, to a fine paste, one heaping teaspoon corn starch, stir into the boiling vinegar until the egg is thoroughly done. Pour this all over the cabbage and set whole on the fire until thoroughly heated, but not boiled. When cold, add yelk of other egg (hard boiled), mixed with the salad oil, and slice the white of the egg over the top. Butter may be used instead of salad oil.

Mrs. E. D. Junkin.

# BREAD.

### Light Bread—No. 1.

Put one yeast cake in a teacup, pour tepid water on to soften it. Do this half an hour before time to set the bread. Take one quart of water, sweet milk or butter milk, either will make good bread. If water is used, let it be as hot as the hand can bear. Stir in sifted flour until a stiff batter is made; stir in the dissolved yeast cake, and beat thoroughly. This sponge should be set at night, and kept in a warm place until morning; then add one small tablespoonful of salt, one-half a teacup of butter, and, if the weather is very warm, a lump of soda as large as a pea, add flour enough to make it stiff; put on the pastry-board and knead until it no longer sticks to the board; set away to rise, which it ought to do in one and one-half hours; then make into four loaves, working each well, and when light, set in the oven to bake. The proper temperature for the oven is such as will allow the hand to be held in it while you can count thirty. Allow one hour for baking. When taken from the oven, rub over the crust with butter, and wrap in several thicknesses of cloth to soften. If properly made and baked, the crust will be thin, and the bread as white and close-grained as sponge cake.

Mrs. J. L. Cunningham.

### Bread—No. 2.

Three quarts flour, one teacup of yeast, one tablespoon of sugar, one teaspoon of soda, two Irish potatoes. Boil the potatoes in water and mash them to a paste, using some of the potato water, then add cold water to make it luke-warm. Sift the flour, salt, sugar and soda together, and mix in the lard. Pour over this the mixture of potatoes and water. If there is not enough to make a soft dough, add more luke-warm water. If you can mold it at all, it is not too soft. Spend at least twenty minutes in kneading, and set to rise after greasing the lump with lard. This prevents a hard crust from forming. When thoroughly light, which will be in about three hours in warm weather, or four or five in cold weather, knead the dough well again and put into greased pans in rolls or loaves for baking. Put the pans in a warm place with a cloth thrown over them an hour longer, then place in an oven to bake. If the oven is in good condition, one hour will be sufficient time for baking. Many people prefer this bread without the potatoes, especially in warm weather.

### Fried Bread.

Cut stale bread into pretty thick slices. Have ready beaten two or three eggs, to which has been added a little salt; dip the slices of bread first in water to moisten them, and afterwards in the egg, then fry in hot lard to a nice brown. Some persons sprinkle on white sugar while hot.

### Fried Bread—No. 2.

Make a thin batter, with a little water, flour and two eggs and a pinch of salt; dip the bread (cut in slices) in the batter, and fry a light brown; if old, let it remain in the batter a few seconds.

### Tea Bread.

Three tumblers of sifted flour, one and one-half teaspoons of cream tartar, half a teaspoonful of soda, tablespoonful of butter, rubbed with the flour, teaspoonful of salt. Mix the cream of tartar with the flour, dissolve the soda in a half tumbler of sweet milk, add this, with a full tumbler of milk, to the butter and flour. Make a soft dough, roll an inch thick, press a saucer upon it, passing a knife around the saucer each time it is pressed to cut the cakes the shape of the saucer. Stick them with a fork, and bake in a quick oven.

### Sour Milk Batter Cakes.

Two cups of sour milk, two cups of flour, one teaspoon of soda, one teaspoon of salt.

### Sally Lunn.

One quart of flour, three eggs, one tablespoonful of butter, one of sugar, add half a cup of good yeast. Mix at 10 o'clock in the morning, and it will be ready to bake for tea. Mix as soft as you can with your hands.

### Flannel Cakes—No. 1.

One quart of flour, two eggs, one and one-half pints boiled milk (used cold), two teaspoons of salt, three tablespoons of yeast. Add the yeast after other ingredients have been mixed. Beat light and set to rise until morning. Bake on a griddle.

### Flannel Cakes—No. 2.

Into a quart of milk, put a tablespoon of butter; set it on the fire and let the butter melt. After it has cooled, add four eggs, well beaten, one and one-half quarts of sifted flour, one teaspoon of salt, one and one-half tablespoons of yeast, or a large yeast cake dissolved in a little milk. Set the batter near the fire to rise, and in three or four hours it will be ready to bake.

### Mississippi Batter Cakes.

Three eggs, one pint of flour, one pint of butter milk, one tablespoon of melted butter. Mix these ingredients, beating the eggs first very light, and set it by the fire to rise two hours; then add a teaspoon of soda, and bake immediately.

### Batter Cakes.

One pint sour milk, one egg and the *yelk* of *one*, one teaspoon of sugar, one of salt; add flour enough to make a batter. Just before baking, stir into the batter a teaspoon of soda, dissolved in a little warm water, and three or four tablespoons of sour cream or one of melted butter improves them.

Nice frttters are made of this by adding flour enough to make a stiff batter, and drop a spoonful into boiling lard.

Mrs. M. A. Davis.

### Beat Biscuit.

Three pints flonr, one tablespoon lard, usual quantity of salt. Make up *very* dry with cold water, and beat until very light, or until the dough blisters.

### Waffles—No. 1.

Two eggs well beaten, one-half pint sweet milk, one quart flour, one teacup cold rice or hominy, one-quarter spoon soda, one-half pint sour milk, or enough to make batter thin enough to pour from a spoon. Grease irons when hot, and bake quickly, butter and serve immediately. If yeast powder is used, leave out sour milk and use sweet milk or water.

### Waffles—No. 2.

One quart sifted flour, two and a half teaspoons baking powder; while dry, add one tablespoon butter, three well beaten eggs, milk or water to make a batter; grease your irons and bake over a moderate fire.    Mrs. E. Warren.

### Waffles—No. 3.

One pint flour, one egg well beaten, one teaspoon baking powder, one tablespoon melted lard or butter, a pinch of salt, milk enough to make a thin batter. Have waffle irons very hot and well greased, and bake quickly. Increase this proportion for a larger amount.    Mrs. F. C. Usher.

### Rice Muffins.

One cup cold boiled rice, three eggs, one tablespoon of butter, a little salt, one teaspoon of yeast powder, add flour to make a thin batter; beat very hard and bake quickly.
   Mrs. E. C. Blake.

### Flour Muffins.

Sift together one quart flour, three teaspoons baking powder and a little salt. Beat two eggs very light, and add to these nearly one pint of milk; stir this into the flour; now add two-thirds cup of butter, or lard, melted without being hot. Have your irons HOT and fill even full. Bake in a moderately hot oven.    M. E. Warren.

### Corn Muffins.

Three cups corn meal, one cup flour, one egg, one-half cup of sugar, two teaspoons cream of tartar, one teaspoon soda, a piece of butter size of a walnut, and enough milk to moisten, Bake quickly.

### Griddle Cakes.

Break up two or three cold biscuits, or as much stale bread, put in a bowl, cover with hot water and let it soak until soft. To this add one pint flour, one egg, a little salt, enough milk or water to make a moderately thick batter, add one heaping teaspoon of baking powder. Bake on a hot griddle until a nice brown. M. E. WARREN.

### Muffins or Sally Lunn.

One-half pint of milk, flour to make a stiff batter, tablespoon of lard, little salt, dessert-spoon of yeast powder. In cold weather, melt the lard in milk.

### Muffins.

Three eggs, one cup of milk, one tablespoon of butter, two teaspoons yeast powder and flour sufficient to make soft batter.

### Biscuit—No. 1.

Three pints flour, one heaping spoon lard, two heaping teaspoons yeast powder, one pinch salt; sift flour, with yeast powder well mixed in; rub lard into flour; make up with water or sweet milk. Knead until smooth and soft; roll and cut. Bake in quick oven.

### Maple Biscuit.

Three eggs, one cup sugar, one tablespoon butter, one-half cup cream or milk, a little yeast powder; add flour until batter is very stiff. Bake in pans as drop biscuit.

### Drop Biscuit.

Beat eight eggs very light, add to them twelve ounces flour and one pound sugar. When perfectly light, drop on tin sheets, or bake in small molds, and quick oven.

MRS. MELTON.

### Graham Biscuit.

One pint sweet milk, one-half cup butter, one-half cup sugar, two eggs, flour enough to make stiff batter, and one teaspoon baking powder. Drop on buttered tins and bake.

### Biscuit—No. 2.

One quart sifted flour, one pinch salt, three heaping teaspoons yeast powder mixed well with flour; add a teaspoon of lard, rubbed well into the flour; mix with sweet milk or water to as soft a consistency as can be rolled. Bake in a quick oven.

### Buttermilk Biscuit.

One teaspoon lard, two cups buttermilk, sift a teaspoon of soda and rub, very fine, one of salt with the flour; add the flour to the buttermilk and lard; pour on the biscuit board and work gently until quite smooth. Bake in a hot oven.

Mrs. J. R. Hutchison.

### Corn Batter Cakes.

One pint cornmeal, three-fourths pint of flour, one even teaspoon of soda, one teaspoon of salt, one and a half quarts of sweet milk, two or three eggs. Have a very hot griddle, and grease with a piece of fat middling. Keep the cook in good humor, have a hot fire, and turn quickly. One quart of water can be substituted in scarcity of milk.

Mrs. E. D. Junkin.

### To Cook Batter Cakes Without Grease.

Tie two tablespoons of salt in a bag and rub over the hot skillet.

### Bread Cakes.

Break the bread into small pieces and soak in cold milk. When soft, add one teaspoon of saleratus, one of salt, and flour for good batter.

### Rice Bread.

One cup of cooked rice, one cup of sifted cornmeal, one cup of milk, one tablespoon of butter, one teaspoon of yeast powder, four eggs.

### Corn Bread.

One pint of meal, mixed very thin with water, three eggs, one tablespoon of lard, one-half tablespoon of butter, one teaspoon of yeast powder, and a little salt. Have the pan greased and hot. Bake in a quick oven. When the meal is fine, it is not necessary to scald it.

### Indian Bannock

One-quart of milk, one pint of corn meal, six eggs, one tablespoon of sugar, a little salt. Scald the milk, and pour on the meal when cool. Add the eggs, beaten separately. Bake in square tins; send to the table in same.

Mrs. E. H. Vincent.

### Hominy Bread.

One and one-half cups of cooked grits, one-half cup of sifted corn meal, one tablespoon of butter, one cup of milk, three eggs, and a little salt. Mix your hominy and milk well, so that it will not be lumpy. Warm the pan and bake in a quick oven.

### Corn Cakes.

One teaspoon of soda dissolved in a quart of butter milk, a pinch of salt, two eggs, one tablespoon of lard, half cup of flour, and enough cornmeal to make a thin batter. Mix well. Very nice.

### Corn Cakes.

One quart cornmeal, one quart of milk, two eggs, one-half cup sugar, or three tablespoons of molasses, one teaspoon of salt, three teaspoons of cream of tartar, one and one-half teaspoons of soda.

### Nice Biscuit.

One quart of flour and two teaspoons of yeast powder evenly stirred through a sieve; add one cup of sweet milk, three tablespoons of butter, and a little salt. Knead and roll thin; cut and bake in *hot* oven.

### Graham Gems.

Three tablespoons of melted butter, three tablespoons of sugar, one teacup of sweet milk, one egg, two or three teaspoons of baking powder, salt to taste. Stir somewhat thicker than griddle cakes. This will fill ordinary gem irons once.

Mrs. James Bailey.

### Genuine Scotch Bread.

Two pounds of flour, one pound of best butter, scant half pound sugar. Work all the salt from the butter; rub butter and sugar to a cream. The flour should be slightly warm. Mix this into the creamed butter evenly and gradually till all

BREAD.

the ingredients are thoroughly mixed. The longer it is kneaded the whiter it will be. Lay it on a biscuit board and press into sheets nearly half an inch thick with the hand (as a rolling-pin has a tendency to toughen it). Cut into squares and bake in a moderate oven till crisp or of a fine yellow brown.

### Split Rolls.

One egg, one tablespoon of sugar, well beaten together, and one yeast cake dissolved in a cup of warm milk; add flour to make a stiff batter; set to rise, then work a heaping tablespoonful of butter, with flour enough to make up the yeast. Roll out the dough an inch thick, spread butter over it, fold the dough over the buttered sides together, and cut out in any shape you fancy. Put them to rise in the pan you bake them in. Bake quickly.

### Plain Bunns.

One tumbler of sweet milk, three eggs, one tablespoonful of butter or lard, six tablespoons of sugar beaten with the eggs till they are light, half a tumbler of good yeast, flour to make a soft dough; set in a warm place to rise; when risen, mold into rolls. After they rise the second time, bake quickly.

### Rusk.

One pint water, one cup baker's yeast. Beat together two tablespoons of butter, one and a half cups of sugar and three eggs. First mix the water, yeast and flour sufficient to make a batter as stiff as can be stirred with a spoon. After standing to rise, add the mixture of eggs, butter and sugar with enough flour to make a soft dough. Knead well, make into rolls, and set to rise. When well risen, bake. For the crust, when brown, mix a little butter, sugar, milk, and the white of one egg, and spread on top.

### Salt Rising Bread.

The earlier in the morning it is set the better. Take one pint of water, one-half teaspoonful of salt and one teaspoonful of sugar. Stir to the thickness of pan cake batter. The water used should be as warm as the hand can bear. Place the vessel containing the batter in warm water, of the temperature of that first used. Let it stand for three hours; in that time water will rise to the surface, then thicken with flour until the batter is as thick as it was at the commencement; let it stand three hours longer, when it will again rise, making a total standing of six hours; then get what flour you need for baking; scald about one pint of it, and after it is cool, mix the rising and flour together, with warm water sufficient to make a dough. Knead on a warm board. A great deal of kneading is required. Place the dough in your baking pan; set aside until it rises to twice its original size, and then bake in a quick oven. Mrs. Abbott.

### Short Cake.

One pint milk, two tablespoons melted butter, one egg, two teaspoons cream of tartar, one teaspoon soda. Put cream of tartar in flour, soda in the milk, mix about the consistency of cup cake. Bake in quick oven.

### Parkin.

Rub one teaspoonful of soda into one pound oatmeal, then add as much treacle as will make it into a stiff dough, adding ginger to taste. Butter a tin, bake in small cakes, flattened by the hand.

### Bunns.

To every quart of flour, twelve spoons of sugar, one egg, a piece of butter the size of two walnuts, mace to your taste.

### Graham Bread.

One quart of tepid water, one teaspoonful of salt, one yeast cake. Stir in flour enough to make a stiff batter. Let it rise over night, then add two-thirds of a cup of molasses. Stir in your graham flour as stiff as you can with an iron spoon. Let the bread rise again, and when light, rub a little lard over the top. Let it bake one hour.

### Potato Yeast Bread.

Sift your flour into a pan or bowl, make a hollow in the middle, drop in your salt, and about the same quantity of sugar. Stir in your yeast, add milk-warm water enough to form a stiff batter. Let it rise, and then knead in as much flour as it will take up, and set it to rise again, then mold it into loaves, and when it is light enough, bake in a moderate oven.                          Mrs. Dixon Lewers.

### Milk Sponge Bread.

Put a pint of boiling water in a pitcher, with a teaspoon of sugar, one-quarter of a teaspoon of salt, and the same of soda. Let it stand until you can bear your fingers in it, then add flour to make a thick batter, and beat it hard for two minutes. Now place the pitcher in a kettle of hot water, not hot enough to scald the mixture; keep the water at the same temperature till the emptyings are light. If set early in the morning, they will be ready if watched carefully at eleven o'clock to make a sponge, the same as for other bread, with a quart of very warm milk. Let this sponge get very light, then make into loaves and set to rise again, taking care they do not get too light this time before putting in the oven, or the bread will be dry and tasteless.

### Boston Brown Bread—No. 1.

Take three teacups of cornmeal, stir into it two cups of boiling sweet milk. When cold, add one teacup of molasses, one cup of wheat flour, and one cup of sour milk. Into the sour milk stir well one teaspoonful of soda, add one-half teaspoonful of salt; steam three hours.

### Boston Brown Bread—No. 2.

One pint of tepid water, two gills of flour, one pint of Indian meal, one-half-pint of molasses, one and a half gills of yeast, one teaspoon of salt, one small teaspoon of carbonate of soda. Mix well, pour into a tall, straight-sided mold, tightly covered. Let it rise three or four hours, steam or boil four or five hours, remove the cover and set in a hot oven to dry. Serve hot in slices.

### Light Bread.

One cup baker's yeast, one cup of water, one tablespoon of mashed Irish potatoes, one teaspoon of salt, one egg, three tablespoons of sugar, three pints of flour. Make a sponge over night by mixing all the ingredients except the flour, adding enough to make a thin dough (almost a batter), cover and set aside until morning, then mix in the rest of the flour. Make into loaves or rolls; let it stand till light. Bake until thoroughly done.        MRS. ROBT. WILSON.

### Boston Brown Bread—No. 3.

Two cups of Indian meal, one cup of wheat flour, one cup of molasses, one pint of sour milk, one cup of warm water, one teaspoon each of salt and soda. Mix the meal, flour, soda and salt, then add the molasses, milk and water. Put in a covered dish and steam four hours, then put in the oven, for a half hour, without the cover.   MRS. C. T. McLELLAND.

### Salt-Rising Bread.

Half a teaspoon of salt, two quarts of warm water. Make the batter thick and set in a warm place to rise. When light and spongy, add a teaspoon of white sugar, one tablespoon of butter. Knead well, mold, and when light, it is ready for the oven.

# YEAST.

### Yeast Cakes.

Take sixteen peach leaves, boil for sometime in water, and strain. There should now be two teacups of water in which the leaves were boiled; if they have boiled down too much, cold water can be added to make two teacupfuls. Thicken with corn meal; add one cup of good yeast. Let stand over night, and until very light, which may not be until nearly noon; then make out into cakes, using as little flour as will hold them together, sprinkle sifted meal over a clean board, and lay the cakes on it to dry. Turn them occasionally, and dry thoroughly *in the shade*—under the stove is a good place, if it never gets warm enough to "scald" them. If dried thoroughly, they will keep any length of time, and always be ready.

If wanted very nice, one can roll the mass on a molding board to half inch thickness and cut out with a biscuit cutter.

Mrs. J. L. Cunningham.

### Yeast Cakes.

Take one pint of tepid water, one teaspoon salt, one tablespoon sugar, one cup baker's yeast, and flour enough to make a stiff batter. Make up over night, and set to rise. Next morning mix with cornmeal and make into a loaf; place in a pan and set to rise again. When light, roll out, cut in small cakes and place in a cool place to dry.

One cake will make two loaves of bread.

### Potato Yeast.

Peel, boil and mash two or three good sized Irish potatoes. Mix with the water in which the potatoes have been boiled, while it is still hot, enough flour to make a thin batter; add the mashed potatoes and let it cool; add one yeast cake, having previously softened it in tepid water, and set it to rise.

### Yeast Cakes.

Take five cents worth of baker's yeast, and enough flour to make a sponge. Set this to rise. When light, stir in a *little* flour, and sufficient Indian meal to enable you to roll out about an inch thick. When rolled out, cut into cakes three inches square, and spread them on shallow pans. Dry them in a shady, airy place, turning them over twice a day while drying When perfectly dry and hard, put them in a bag, tie them up, and keep in a cool place.

When used for bread, soak in luke warm water until soft. One cake will be sufficient for three or four loaves of bread.

### Dry Hop Yeast.

Boil a small handful of hops in three pints of water; strain and add while boiling hot, a teacup of flour, stirring until quite smooth, then add one tablespoon sugar and one teaspoon of ginger. When cool, stir in thoroughly one cup of yeast. Place in a warm place to rise. When very light, thicken with corn meal. Make into small cakes and dry, turning them frequently. They are better to dry quickly, though care should be taken not to scald them.

One of these yeast cakes soaked in a cup of warm water will make one large or two small loaves of bread.

### Yeast that will not Sour.

Take a handful of hops; of these, make a tea, adding sufficient water to make a gallon. Boil twelve Irish potatoes; mash them and add to the water, with a teacup of salt, a teacup of sugar, and a tablespoon of ginger.

Use a cupful of this yeast to three quarts of flour.

### Potato Yeast.

One handful of hops, two quarts water, four large potatoes, one tablespoon salt, one cup brown sugar. Boil the hops and water together. Pare, grate and scald the potatoes, adding a little salt and sugar. When cool, add the yeast and bottle, Keep in a cool place. Mrs. James Bailey.

## Yeast.

Boil one handful of hops and two of wheat bran with two quarts of water for twenty minutes. Take off the fire and stir in quickly, while boiling hot, as much wheatflour as will make a thick batter. Let this mixture stand until luke warm, then add one tablespoon each of sugar, salt and ginger (either powdered or extract), also one cup of yeast. Let this stand in a warm place until it has fermented; pour into a stone jug and cork, at first, slightly, but, after fermentation ceases, cork tightly and keep in a cool place.

# VEGETABLES.

After washing and peeling, lay them into cold water for a while before cooking. Let the water be boiling when they are put in, and don't let it stop. Boil turnips from forty to sixty minutes; beets, at least one hour; spinach, one hour and a half; parsnips, from twenty to thirty minutes; onions, in several waters until tender; green corn, twenty to thirty minutes; green peas, twenty minutes, and in but little water; asparagus, same as peas; winter squash, twenty to forty minutes, in but little water; cabbage, thirty to sixty minutes, and salt while boiling.

### Cabbage a la Cauliflower.

Cut the cabbage fine as for slaw, put it into a stew-pan, cover with water and keep closely covered. When tender, drain off the water, put in a piece of butter with a little salt, one-half cup of sweet cream, or one cup of milk. Leave on the stove a few minutes before serving.

### Corn Fritters.

To a can of corn, add two eggs well beaten, two tablespoons of flour, one teaspoon of salt, one-half teaspoon of pepper. Mix thoroughly, have the pan hot, put in two tablespoons of lard, and drop in the corn in large spoonfuls; cook brown.

### Stuffed Tomatoes with Shrimps.

Twelve large tomatoes, six soda crackers one pint shrimps, one small onion, one large spoonful of butter. Take out the meat of the tomatoes, leaving the outside whole in order to stuff. Roll the crackers very fine, and mix with the meat of the tomatoes. Boil the shrimps, pick and chop them, and mix with the tomatoes and crackers. Chop the onion with a small sprig of parsley; add the butter, with salt and pepper to taste. Fill the skins of the tomatoes with this mixture; grate crackers over the top and bake.

### Green Corn Fritters.

Grate six ears of boiled corn, beat the yelks of three eggs, and mix with the corn; add two even tablespoons of flour, season with pepper and salt, add the whites of three eggs beaten to a stiff froth. Fry in hot lard; serve upon a napkin laid on a flat dish.
Mrs. D. C. Smith.

### Corn Oysters.

To one can of corn, add two eggs, flour enough for a thick batter, salt and pepper to taste. Fry in hot lard like fritters.

### Baked Tomatoes—No. 1.

Prepare just as you would for stewing, put into a pudding dish and bake. Serve in the dish in which they are cooked.

### Stewed Tomatoes.

To a can of tomatoes, add one tablespoon of sugar, and a heaping tablespoon of butter, a few pieces of bread, broken in, salt and pepper to taste. Stew until well thickened.

### Baked Tomatoes—No. 2.

Cut in slices, good, fresh tomatoes (not too ripe), put a layer of them in a dish suitable for baking, then a layer of bread crumbs over them, salt, pepper and plenty of butter, another layer of tomatoes, and so on, until the dish is full. Bake one hour.

### Fried Tomatoes—No. 1.

Take nice, fresh tomatoes, wash them and slice without peeling, as you would for the table. Dip each slice in sifted flour and sprinkle with salt. Fry in hot lard on a deep griddle, turning each slice as you would griddle cakes. Serve on a flat dish and spinkle white sugar over each layer of tomatoes while hot. This is an excellent breakfast dish.
Mrs. E. D. Junkin.

### Fried Tomatoes—No 2.

Do not pare them, but cut in slices; dip in cracker pounded and sifted, and fry in a little good butter.

## VEGETABLES.

### To Broil Tomatoes.

Take large, round tomatoes, wash and wipe, and put them on a gridiron over live coals, the stem side down. When brown, turn them, and let them cook till quite hot through. Place them on a hot dish and send quickly to the table, when each one may season for himself with pepper salt and butter.

### Tomatoes Baked Whole.

Take large, thoroughly ripe tomatoes; put in a baking-dish without anything else. Bake until the skins shrivel. Season with salt, pepper, and a tablespoonful of butter, and serve hot.

### Sweet Potatoes.

Sweet potatoes require more time for cooking than Irish potatoes. To boil, take large, fine potatoes, wash clean, boil with the skins on in plenty of water, without salt. They will be done in about an hour, then drain off the water and set them for a few minutes before the fire or in the oven, that they may be well dried. Peel, or not, as you prefer, before sending to table. They are nice mashed, after boiling, seasoned with salt, pepper and butter. Put into a dish and bake until brown.

### Fried Sweet Potatoes.

For this purpose may be used potatoes that are too large for baking well. Cut in slices one-fourth of an inch thick, and sprinkle with salt. Have a well greased frying pan hot, put in the potatoes and fry a light brown. Be careful not to cook too rapidly, lest the potatoes blister and do not cook thoroughly. Some persons prefer to boil the potatoes half done before slicing for frying.

### Very Nice Sweet Potatoes.

Boil potatoes thoroughly, peel and mash well, add one tablespoonful each of butter and sugar and three eggs. Beat well, put in a dish and bake.

### Baked Sweet Potatoes—No. 1.

Peel the potatoes and cut in slices one-fourth of an inch in thickness. Place a layer of these slices in a baking dish, over this put a thin layer of butter and sugar. Proceed in this

## VEGETABLES.

way until the dish is full, add sufficient water to moisten the sugar. Bake in a moderate oven, let them remain until the syrup is thick and the potatoes thoroughly done. A grated nutmeg or a sliced lemon may be added.

### Baked Sweet Potatoes—No. 2.

Select nice, medium-sized yams, wash well, and put in a hot oven. Turn them occasionally to prevent cooking unequally. Bake until soft through.

### Baked Sweet Potatoes—No. 3.

With a fresh pork roast, take sweet potatoes, peel and cut in half, and bake with the meat. Serve with some of the gravy.

### Boiled Sweet Potatoes.

Boil the potatoes in their skins until soft, peel and pour melted butter over them. When potatoes are new, before they become sweet and juicy, this way of cooking them is preferable to baking.

### Boiled Irish Potatoes.

Boil in the skins until quite done; pour off the water and allow them to dry for a few minutes. Serve either in the skins or remove the skins; sprinkle with salt and pepper, and pour over them melted butter.

### Fried Irish Potatoes Cakes.

Boil till done, peel and wash, seasoning with salt and pepper to the taste. Make into small, round, flat cakes and flour on each side. Have in a frying-pan lard boiling hot. Fry the cakes crisp and brown.

These may be made of cold potatoes left from previous meals.

### Saratoga Potatoes.

Peel and slice on a slaw-cutter into cold water, wash thoroughly and drain, spread between the folds of a clean cloth, rub and pat until dry. Fry a few at a time in boiling lard, salt as you take out.

Saratoga potatoes are often eaten cold. They can be prepared three or four hours before needed, and if kept in a warm place they will be crisp and nice. Can be used for garnishing game and steak.

### To Boil Irish Potatoes.

Peel and put in a pot with sufficient well-salted cold water to cover them, boil till nearly done, then take out with a skimmer and put in a colander over a pot half full of boiling water. Keep covered, and serve as soon as possible.

Mrs. D. C. Smith.

### Mashed Irish Potatoes—No. 1.

Boil till quite done, peel and mash, with half cup of milk and large spoon of butter. Season with salt and pepper.

### Baked Irish Potatoes.

Boil till done, peel and mash; add salt and pepper, a large spoon of butter and two eggs, put in baking dish and bake to light brown.

### Roasted Irish Potatoes.

Put the potatoes in a moderately hot oven; bake until the skins shrivel.

### Fried Irish Potatoes.

Take cold boiled potatoes, slice in thin slices, sprinkle with salt. In a hot, well-greased frying-pan, fry them to a light brown.

### Mashed Irish Potatoes—No. 2.

Wash and cut in halves or quarters, put into boiling water and boil half an hour, pour off all the water, add salt and mash them until perfectly smooth, then add cream, if you have it; if not, milk; and beat well with a fork or spoon. The beating makes it light.

### Potatoes a la Maitre d' Hotel.

The first Bermuda potatoes should be cooked *à la maitre d' hotel*. It must be remembered that *new* potatoes, being immature, *require thorough cooking*. Boil the potatoes beforehand, then slice. Then take as follows: One pint of milk, one tablespoonful of butter, one teaspoonful of flour, one tablespoonful of chopped parsley, a little salt and white pepper. Use the flour to thicken the milk. Boil all these ingredients so as to get them smooth, then put in the sliced potatoes, give a final boil and serve.

### To Cook New Potatoes.

Scrape well and boil till done, putting a little salt in the water. When sufficiently cooked, pour off the water. Have a piece of butter the size of an egg, roll in a little flour, and stir with the potatoes while hot. Add a little pepper and a cupful of cream.

### A Nice Breakfast Dish—No. 1.

Cut cold boiled Irish potatoes into small cubes. Heat to boiling a half-cup of milk, with a tablespoon of butter, then put in the potatoes, with a sprinkle of flour, and season with salt and pepper. Let the potatoes become heated thoroughly, and serve hot.

### A Nice Breakfast Dish—No. 2.

Into a frying pan, put a tablespoon of butter; when quite hot, add six cold boiled potatoes, which have been quartered and cut in thick slices; let the potatoes become quite hot, but not brown, add half a cup of milk, salt and pepper to taste. Stir constantly, and when thickened, serve. A few sprigs of parsley will improve both dishes.

### Squash.

Peel and quarter three common sized squash, cover with water, and let them boil until perfectly tender. Drain off the water, pour them into a bowl, add, when nearly cool, three eggs, one tablespoon of sugar, one tablespoon of butter, a little salt, enough flour to make a thick batter, and fry in hot lard.

Egg plants are very nice prepared in the same way.

Mrs. E. C. Blake.

### Boiled Onions.

Skin them thoroughly; put them to boil. When they have boiled a few minutes, pour off the water and add clear, cold water, and then set them to boil again. Pour this water off and add more cold water, when they may boil until done. This will make them white and clear, and very mild in flavor. After they are done, pour off all the water and add a little cream or milk and let it remain until heated thoroughly. Season with salt and pepper.

### Boston Baked Beans.

Put a quart of beans to soak over night. In the morning, pour off the water, and add fresh water enough to cover, to which add one tablespoon of molasses. Put a small piece of salt pork in the centre, almost covering it with beans. Bake slowly six or eight hours. Add hot water, as needed, until nearly done, when they may be cooked dry or moist according to taste.

### To Fry Ochra.

Boil a quart, strain off the water, mash it smooth, salt and pepper it, beat in two eggs, add one-half tumbler of flour to make the batter stiff enough to fry as fritters.

Mrs. D. C. Smith.

### Celery.

Wash the stems clean in salt and water, then drop them into boiling water. Boil twenty minutes, take up and drain. Place some toasted bread in a dish; lay the celery over it, and season with butter, pepper and salt. L. Barrett.

### Parsnip Fritters.

Four parsnips boiled and mashed fine; add three well-beaten eggs, two tablespoons of sifted flour, butter the size of an egg, one teacup of milk, and salt to taste. Upon a hot, buttered griddle drop the mixture, and bake after the style of flannel cakes. Serve quite hot.

### Parsnip Stew.

Three slices of salt pork; boil one and one-half hours. Scrape five large parsnips, cut in quarters lengthwise, add to the pork, and let boil one-half hour, then add a few potatoes, and let all boil together until the potatoes are soft. The fluid in the kettle should be about a cupful when ready to take off.

### To Prepare Egg Plant.

Boil the egg plants until they are tender, cut them in quarters, scrape them, leaving the skin, and put the dressing in, made as follows: To the scraped-out center of three large egg plants, add three eggs, two slices of bread, one pod of red pepper, one heaping tablespoon of butter, and salt to the taste; chop all together very fine, put it back in the skin, and bake until it is brown. MRS. WM. CHRISTIAN.

### Spinach.

Spinach requires good washing and close picking. Boil twenty minutes in boiling water, drain, season with butter, pepper and salt. Garnish the dish with slices of hard boiled eggs.

### Scalloped Parsnips.

Mash one pint of boiled parsnips, add two tablespoons of butter, one teaspoon of salt, a little pepper, two teaspoons of cream. Mix all the ingredients well, put over the fire and stew until the mixture bubbles, then turn into a buttered dish, cover with bread crumbs, dot with butter and brown in the oven.

### Baked Egg Plant.

Cut in halves, scrape out the center, leaving with the skin about one-third of an inch; chop the inside of the egg plant very fine, add two ripe tomatoes, one onion, some bread crumbs, a little parsley, and green pepper (onion and pepper to be chopped separately, very fine), salt, butter, and very little pepper. Mix very smooth, put in the shell, butter on top, and bake about one-half hour.

### Turnips.

Pare and cut into pieces, put them into boiling water, well salted, and boil until tender. Drain thoroughly, and then mash, and add a piece of butter, pepper and salt to taste, and a small teaspoon of sugar. Stir until they are thoroughly mixed, and serve hot.

### Asparagus.

Cook only the tender green stalks, cut them of equal lengths, and boil in water, with a little salt, till tender. While the asparagus is cooking, prepare some nicely toasted bread, lay the asparagus on the toast, and season with butter, salt and pepper. Prepare some drawn butter and pour over all.

## VEGETABLES.

### Succotash.

Boil butter beans half an hour, salt them sufficiently, then add half as much green corn. Cook till done, then add butter and season to taste.

### Ochra and Tomatoes.

Use equal quantities of each, slice the ochra and skin the tomatoes. Stew without water three-quarters of an hour, then add butter, salt and pepper.

### To Cook Green Peas.

Put water enough on the peas to almost cover them, season with salt and boil fifteen or twenty minutes, then add a cupful of cream and a little butter; thicken slightly with a little flour and water mixed to a smooth paste.

### Boiled Hominy.

Soak one cup of fine hominy in three cups of water and salt to taste. In the morning, turn it into a quart pail; put the pail into a kettle of boiling water, cover tightly and steam one hour. Add one teacup of sweet milk, and boil fifteen minutes.

### Rice Omelet.

One teacup of boiled rice, one teacup of water, three eggs, well beaten, one teaspoon of butter. Season with grated ham, a little minced onion, pepper and salt. Bake a light brown.

Mrs. D. C. Smith.

### To Cook Beets.

Let them boil until tender. When done, place them in a bowl of cold water, and remove the skin with the hands. Slice them, and serve hot, with butter and sugar, or cold, with vinegar.

### Beans.

String beans should be boiled with bacon. They should be boiled three or four hours, until quite tender.

Boil butter beans in salt water.

### Cashaw—No. 1.

Peel and slice in thin slices, and fry as you would sweet potatoes.

VEGETABLES.

### Cashaw—No. 2.

Peel and cut in slices one and one-half inches, and stew until quite tender, with butter, sugar and water. Cook until the syrup becomes thick.

### Cashaw—No. 3.

Cut off the end of the cashaw, take out the seeds and fill it with sugar, butter and grated nutmeg, replace the end, and bake. It will require three or four hours baking.

### To Cook Cornfield Peas.

Go to the pea-patch early in the morning and gather the peas, take them home in a split basket. Take them in the left hand and gouge them out with your right thumb until it gets sore, then reverse hands. Look the pea well in the eye to see its color, but cook them anyway, as no color exempts the pea from domestic service, still the grey eye and white lips and cheeks are to be preferred. Throw the shelled peas mercilessly into hot water and boil them until they "cave in." When you see they are well subdued, take them out and fry them about ten minutes in gravy—a plenty of gravy, good fat meat gravy, and try to induce the gravy to marry and become social with the peas. When you see that the union is complete, so that no man can put them asunder, and would not wish to if he could, put them in a dish and eat them all.

Hon. J. C. Hutcheson.

# OMELETS AND EGGS.

### An Omelet.

It is an easy thing to do, and not often well done. The trouble lies in the fact that most cooks overbeat their eggs. A simple omelet is not a soufflé. Break all the eggs into one plate, *stir* rather than *beat* them, and to each three eggs used, put in *one* teaspoon cold water   I do not like milk. Salt and pepper the eggs moderately (American cooks use too much pepper), take some parsley and chop it. Let the parsley be fine—fine (American cooks never chop parsley fine enough), put two ounces of sweet butter in your pan—lard for an omelet is an abomination. When the butter is *very* hot, pour in the eggs; the instant that it is cooked on one side (*not crisp*, but simply *cooked*), turn it quickly and cook the other side. Double it over when you serve it, on a very hot plate. The cold water used makes the omelet light and moist.

### Plain Omelet.

Separate six eggs and beat very light the whites to a stiff froth, add to the yelks a small cupful of milk, pepper and salt to taste, and then stir in the whites lightly. Put a lump of butter in a hot frying pan; when it melts, pour in the mixture gently and set over a clear fire. It should not remain over the fire more than ten minutes. If there is danger of burning, slip a broad-bladed knife under the omelet to prevent this. When done, lay a hot dish over the top of the frying pan and turn out so the browned side of the omelet will be uppermost.          Mrs. D. C. Smith.

### Parsley and Eggs.

Take ten fresh eggs, break and beat them until light. Have ready some tender young parsley chopped fine, stir this into the eggs until the mixture is thick. Have a well greased frying pan hot; into this pour the mixture, and stir until done, seasoning with salt and pepper.

### Egg Omelet.

One ounce of bread crumbs, soaked in half a pint of milk, four eggs, salt and pepper to taste. Mix well together, pour into a small pan well buttered. Bake in the oven until nicely browned.

### Stuffed Eggs.

Chop fine one dozen oysters, mix with them the beaten yelk of an egg, thicken with toasted bread crumbs, add one tablespoon of cream, and salt and pepper to taste, fill the shells and bake in a covered pan half an hour.

### Stuffed Eggs.

Boil the eggs hard, cut in half, remove the meat and chop it fine, add butter, cream, salt and pepper to taste, fill each half shell and set them in a pan and bake to a nice brown.

### Stuffed Eggs.

Boil some eggs hard, remove the shells, and cut them in half lengthwise, take out the yelks, mash them fine and season with butter, pepper and salt, chop some cold boiled ham fine and mix with the yelks, fill the halved whites with this mixture and put them in a pan, set in the oven and brown slightly.

### Poached Eggs.

Have ready a pan over the fire containing boiling water about an inch in depth. Break the eggs in separately. Let them remain until the whites are hard. Be careful to allow them small space, otherwise the whites will spread, and not look well.

### Baked Eggs.

Butter a clean smooth baking-dish, break as many eggs as will be needed into a saucer, one at a time—if found good—slip it into the dish. Use none with broken yelks, nor must they be crowded enough to break when put in the dish. Put a small piece of butter on each one, and sprinkle with salt and pepper. Set in a well-heated oven, and bake till the whites are set. If the oven is properly heated it will take but a few minutes. These are more delicate than fried eggs.

### A very Nice way to Poach Eggs.

In your pan of boiling water place as many muffin rings as you have eggs to poach; break an egg in each ring separately. Let them cook until the whites are hard. Serve on hot buttered toast.

### Hard Boiled Eggs.

Place the eggs in boiling water; let them remain five minutes, when when they will be ready to serve.

A very pretty dinner dish is to remove the shells from hard boiled eggs, cut them in half and place them in a dish, then sprinkle over them a little salt and pepper, and pour melted butter over the whole.

### Soft Boiled Eggs.

Put the eggs in boiling water for three minutes only.

### Fried Eggs.

Have ready a frying-pan of boiling lard. Break each egg in separately, sprinkle as they fry, with a little salt and pepper. These are very nice served on fried ham or breakfast bacon.

### Scrambled Eggs.

Have a frying-pan hot and well greased; break the eggs all together in a pan, then pour them into the hot frying pan and stir until done, seasoning with salt and pepper.

### Pickled Eggs.

Boil hard whatever number of fresh eggs you wish to pickle and lay in cold water. Peel off the shells, and lay in a stone jar, adding mace, cloves and nutmegs. Fill the jar with boiling vinegar. They will be ready for use in two days.

## SIDE DISHES.

### To Make Macaroni.

Take the whites of three eggs, add sufficient flour to make a stiff dough, and a little salt. Roll as thin as a knife blade, cut into small strips and cook in boiling water. When done, take it out and serve with butter, salt and pepper.

Mrs. Wm. Christian.

### Macaroni with Cheese.

Throw into boiling water some macaroni, with salt according to quantity used, let it boil one-quarter of an hour, when it will be a little more than half cooked. Drain off the water, place the macaroni in a sauce-pan with milk to cover, boil till done. Butter a pudding dish, sprinkle the bottom with plenty of grated cheese. Put in the macaroni a little white pepper, plenty of butter, sprinkle on more cheese, cover with bread crumbs, or use it without them if preferred. Set in a quick oven to brown. Serve hot.

### Macaroni Pudding to be Eaten with Meat.

One cup macaroni, broken in pieces an inch long, and boiled in salt water until tender. Take from the water and place in a pudding dish, over which pour one pint of milk, in which has been mixed two well beaten eggs and one cup of grated cheese. Bake thirty minutes.

Mrs. E. O'Donohue, Chicago.

### A Nice Relish for Supper.

One pint of grated cheese, one pint of bread crumbs, two well beaten eggs, half grated nutmeg, one teaspoon of salt. Heat a pint of sweet milk boiling hot, with a large spoonful of butter, pour this over the other ingredients and mix well; cover and set back on the fire for three or four hours, stirring occasionally. Half an hour before supper, butter a pie plate, pour the mixture into it, set in the oven and brown. It should not cook while on the fire, but merely dissolve. Serve hot.     Mrs. Connell.

### Welsh Rarebit.

Three eggs to about one-half pound of cheese, a piece of butter the size of a walnut, mustard, pepper, sugar and salt to taste. Whip the eggs light, add the cheese, and beat well together.     Mrs. Judge Thomson.

### A Nice Breakfast Dish.

Take a little bacon gravy or a spoonful of butter, put in a hot frying pan, pour in some molasses and let it boil a few minutes. Serve hot.

### A Nice Way to Serve Cheese.

Put a cup of grated cheese in half a pint of milk and boil until the cheese softens into the milk. Stir frequently, then add two eggs well beaten, season to taste, and stir rapidly for a few minutes, then take from the fire and spread over slices of nicely browned toast, and serve *very* hot.

# COFFEE, TEA AND CHOCOLATE.

### Coffee.

To one teacup of fresh ground coffee, add one egg and water enough to wet the coffee, stir together, then add three pints of boiling water. Let it come to a boil, then set aside where it will keep warm.  Mrs. D. C. Smith.

### Mock Cream for Coffee.

If you cannot procure milk, beat the yelks of eggs very light, and add a little white sugar. Put some in a cup, and while pouring coffee stir all the time; or, to a pint of milk, beat up thoroughly the yelks and stir in the milk.

### Dripped Coffee.

One cup of coffee; grind and put in the dripper. Put the coffee pot where it will get warm, pour four cups of boiling water gradually over the coffee. This will make three cups of strong coffee. Serve with boiling milk.

### Good Coffee.

Allow a heaping tablespoonful of coffee grounds to every cup of coffee desired. First moisten with water, or, better, the white of an egg; add cold water and bring to a vigorous boil.

### Mock Cream for Tea or Coffee.

To a pint of milk, take the yelk of one egg, beat thoroughly, put on the fire and let it come to a scald. Is improved by adding a little cream when cold.

### Chocolate—No. 1.

Grate two ounces Baker's chocolate; add to this a cup of sugar. Put in a sauce-pan, with two tablespoons of water; stir a few moments until smooth. Pour in gradually one pint of boiling water, one pint of milk. Let all boil one minute, then dissolve a small teaspoon of corn starch in a little cold water, and add to the chocolate. Allow all to boil one minute before serving.

### Chocolate—No. 2.

To one ounce of Baker's chocolate allow one pint of milk or one-half pint each of milk and water. Let the milk come to a boil. Have the chocolate grated, and mix with it sufficient sugar to sweeten the whole. When the milk boils, stir in the chocolate and let it boil until smooth. One square of Baker's chocolate is one ounce.

### Tea.

One teaspoonful of tea for each person, and one spoonful extra will make *strong* tea. Pour a very little boiling water (be sure it is bubbling) at first. Let it stand five minutes or less, and then add boiling water sufficient for the table.

It is impossible to give directions for tea-making to suit all persons, there being such a diversity of taste as to strength. It is a good plan, however, to make strong tea, and provide yourself with a small pitcher of boiling water, with which you may weaken it to each individual taste.

# PIES AND PASTRY.

### Good Pie Crust.

One quart flour, one-half pound lard, one teaspoonful salt, mix the ingredients thoroughly, using only the tips of the fingers. Add enough cold water to make a dough as soft as can be easily handled. Get it into a lump on the pastry board, being careful to handle very lightly. Do not knead, but cut it in two parts and place one on top of the other, press slightly with the palm of the hand. Do this repeatedly until it becomes smooth. Roll very thin. This will make three or four pies of large size.    Mrs. J. R. Hutchison.

### Puff Paste.

The well-beaten whites of three eggs, three tablespoons cold water, mix it with one pound of butter, and then add flour until it is stiff enough to roll.    Mrs. G. A. McDonell.

### Pie Crust.

Allow one cup of flour and a large spoonful of lard to each covered pie of ordinary size, sift the flour and take out a handful for rolling out, add a pinch of salt for each pie. Put your lard into the flour in lumps as large as an almond, but do not rub, as every lump will make it flaky. Work in as much cold water as will make a dough just soft enough to roll easily. Handle as little as possible. Roll the crust very thin and bake in a quick oven, and you will surely have good pie crust.

For meat pies, use less shortening and put in a little yeast powder.

### Lemon Pie—No. 1.

Three lemons, one pound of sugar, one-fourth pound of butter, nine eggs, one pint of milk. Mix the butter and sugar, add the grated peel and juice of the lemons, with a tablespoonful of corn starch or flour. Beat the eggs separately. Just before putting in the whites of the eggs, stir in the milk. Mix well, and bake immediately. One crust. This makes three pies.

### Lemon Pie—No 2.

Three lemons, one teacupful of raisins, one and one-half cups of molasses. Take the juice of the lemons, chop the peel and the raisins both very fine, mix with the molasses, stir well, and add a little flour and water. Bake in a rich paste. This makes two pies.

### Lemon Custard Pie.

Three eggs, two cups of sugar, four soda crackers, pounded, one and one-half cups of milk, three lemons. Beat the yelks of the eggs with sugar, add the crackers and milk, then the grated rind and juice of the lemons. Bake in one crust.

### Lemon Pie—No. 3.

Two lemons, five eggs, two cups of sugar, one and one-half biscuits, dissolved in water, one cup of sweet milk. Mix with common sense, and bake accordingly.

### Silver Pie.

One lemon, one large white potato, one egg, one cup of white sugar, one cup of cold water. Peel and grate the potato, add the juice and rind of the lemon, the beaten white of the egg, and the sugar and water. Bake in one paste. After baking, spread on the top the whites of three eggs, frothed, sweetened and flavored withl emon. Set again in the oven to brown. Lay on small pieces of jelly or jam just before taking to the table.

### Lemon Pie—No. 4.

Four lemons, four cups of sugar, yelks of twelve eggs, one teaspoon of butter, one cup af sweet milk, one cracker, rolled fine. Mix the grated rind and juice of the lemons with the sugar, beat thoroughly, add the butter, milk and cracker, and the yelks of the eggs. Beat the whites of the eggs to a froth, add three tablespoons of white sugar, flavor with lemon. When the pies are done spread this over the top and bake a light brown.

### Lemon Pie—No. 5.

Two lemons, two eggs, two teacups of white sugar, two tablespoons of butter, two tablespoons of corn starch, two cups of boiling water. Dissolve the corn starch in cold water, then add the two cups of boiling water, put over the fire and boil until clear and thick, stirring constantly; add the butter, sugar and the grated rind and juice of the lemons. Beat the eggs thoroughly, and add to the mixture. Bake with an upper and under crust. A few raisins added is a great improvement. This makes two pies.

### Orange Puffs.

Put into a sauce-pan one pint of milk, two teaspoons of gelatine, the beaten yelks of five eggs, the pulp, juice and peel of two oranges, six tablespoons of sugar, and one tablespoon of butter; stir over the fire until it thickens, then take out the peel and pour the custard into patty-pans lined with paste, and bake. While baking, beat up the whites of the eggs with four tablespoons of white sugar. When the puffs are nearly done spread this over the top of each and set them in the oven to brown.

### Irish Potato Custard.

Mix three-fourths of a pound of butter with one pound of boiled Irish potatoes previously run through a sieve. Beat the yelks of six eggs and the whites of three with three-fourths pound of sugar, and add them to the butter and potato, together with one nutmeg and two tablespoons of orange peel, also add one wine-glass of brandy and wine mixed. Bake in a rich crust.

### Lemon Custard.

Grate the rind of four lemons, squeeze the juice, add four teacups of sugar, the yelks of six eggs well beaten, two teacups of milk, four tablespoonfuls of corn-starch or arrowroot beaten well together. This makes three common-sized pies;

no upper crust. When done, have ready the six whites, beaten to a stiff froth, with four tablespoons of powdered sugar, spread on the pies, replace in the oven for three minutes, until they are a light brown.

### Lemon Puffs.

Made exactly as orange puffs, with the exception of using eight instead of six tablespoons of sugar, and leaving out the pulp of the lemons.

### Buttermilk Custard—No. 1.

Set a gallon of milk on the fire, and when the whey rises, pour all into a bag to drip. To the curd, add three eggs, one-half pound sugar, one-half pound butter, flavor to taste, and bake in a crust.

### Buttermilk Custard—No. 2.

Beat together a heaping cup of sugar and four eggs, add one-half cup butter, beat thoroughly, and add one and a half pints of buttermilk. Line the pie tins with crust, slice an apple thin and lay in each pie. Fill the crust with the mixture and bake with no upper crust. MRS. L. M. NOBLE.

### Lemon Custard.

Two lemons, four eggs, one tablespoon of butter, nearly a teacup of water and about two of sugar. Will make two custards.

### Jelly Custard.

Three eggs, one cup of sugar, one cup of jelly, one tablespoonful of butter, lemon and spice to the taste. This must be baked with only an under crust. MRS. J. D. SAYERS.

### Cream Custard.

Two eggs, one cup of cream, one cup of sugar, one tablespoon of butter, two tablespoons of flour, season with nutmeg and orange-flower water, and add very thinly sliced citron. Bake in a crust. MRS. J. D. SAYERS, Bastrop.

### Apple Custard Pie.

Scald the milk, let it cool, grate some apples; to each cup of apples, have two-thirds cup powdered sugar, four well beaten eggs, one cup milk, nutmeg or cinnamon to taste. Line a pie dish with rich crust, let it bake, then fill with the custard and let the whole bake. To be served cold.

### Citron Custard.

The yelks of seven eggs, with one white, one-fourth pound of sugar, and pounded orange peel to taste. Bake in a rich pastry. Line the pastry with thin slices of citron, rolled in flour and pour the custard over it.

### Cocoanut Pudding.

One quart milk, one cup bread crumbs toasted and soaked in the milk, one small cocoanut grated, three eggs, sweeten to taste, spread slices of oranges on top and bake.

### Mock Mince Pie.

One cup raisins, one cup currants, one cup citron, one cup sugar, one cup molasses, one cup bread crumbs or crackers, one-half cup butter, one cup vinegar and water, spices, allspice, cloves and cinnamon. Bake with top crust.

### Jelly Pie.

One cup jelly, two cups sugar, four eggs, one-half cup butter. Cream the sugar and butter, beat the yelks until very light and mix with the sugar and butter, then add the whites, and, last, the jelly. Flavor to suit the taste

Mrs J. R. Hutchison.

### Apple Pie—No. 1.

Stew one pound of apples with a stick of cinnamon, half dozen cloves and some lemon peel. When soft, sweeten to your taste. Press them through a sieve, and add the well-beaten yelks of four eggs, three-fourths of a pound of butter, and peel and juice of one lemon. Mix well, and bake one-half hour in puff paste. Very good.

Mrs. G. A. McDonell.

### Apple Pie—No. 2.

One quart stewed apples, four eggs, one cup milk, two cups sugar, one-half cup butter, one lemon. Stew the rind of lemon with the apple. Bake without top crust.

### Peach Cobbler.

Make pastry same as for pie, line a deep dish with it. Peel peaches and cut them in quarters; fill up the dish; put in one cup water; put top crust on and bake. When done, take top crust off, and place in dish in which it will be served; add to peaches two cups sugar, one cup butter, and nutmeg to taste; pour peaches on crust in dish, take out bottom crust and place on top, sprinkle with sugar.  MRS. J. R. HUTCHISON.

### Strawberry Short Cake.

One quart flour, one teaspoon salt, two teaspoons yeast powder, three tablespoons butter, one egg, two tablespoons white sugar, one-half pint milk. Sift the flour, powder and salt together, rub in the butter, add the egg, slightly beaten, then the sugar and milk, and mix into a smooth dough, soft enough to be easily handled. Roll out in two pieces to size required, lay one on top of the other and bake in hot oven, in a well greased pan, about fifteen minutes, and separate while warm, not hot. Use one for bottom crust, cover with a layer of berries, then lay on the other piece and cover as before. Serve with powdered sugar and cream.

MRS. J. R. HUTCHISON.

### Green Apple Pie.

Grate six apples, one cup of sugar, three tablespoons butter, four eggs, a little lemon juice, a few currants, and little spice. Bake with no upper crust. One or two teaspoons of brandy may be added.  MRS. G. A. MCDONELL.

### Orange Pie.

Three oranges, two teacups sugar, one-fourth teacup butter, one teacup sifted flour, three eggs well beaten. Mix eggs, butter, sugar and flour, then add pulp and juice of oranges with grated peeling, and one orange to season with. Beat butter, sugar and eggs until very light.

MRS. FANNIE NOBLE.

### Washington Pie.

One cup of sugar, one-half cup of butter, one-half cup of sweet milk, one teaspoon of yeast powder, two cups of flour, one well beaten egg. Beat all well together and flavor with nutmeg. Bake in two round tins, turn one of the cakes bottom upwards on a plate and spread over it peach jelly, or any that you prefer, lay the other cake upon it, frost, or sift over it powdered sugar. Mrs. Milton.

### Sweet Potato Pie—No. 1.

Boil the potatoes; when done, strain, add one cup sugar, two cups milk, one-half cup butter, five eggs, a little nutmeg. Bake with bottom crust. Irish potatoes can be used in the same way.

### Mince Pies.

Four pounds of lean beef, two pounds fresh beef suet, then add two pounds brown sugar, two ounces ground spices, mixed in equal proportions, grated rind of six lemons, one pint brandy, one pint wine, two pounds raisins, two pounds currants, two pounds citron. Chop the raisins with six apples, add the other fruit to the mixture, with two teaspoons of salt, Stir all well together. Boil meat and chop fine.
Mrs. E. C. Blake.

### Cracker Pie.

Three cups of rolled cracker, one cup of butter, three cups of sugar, one cup of milk. Flavor to taste.

### Molasses Pies.

Take six eggs, beat separately, take a pint cup, fill two-thirds with molasses, then fill up with sugar, spice to the taste, or season with lemon before putting the mixture into the crust, put a lump of butter in the size of an egg. Bake slowly in crust. Mrs. T. C. Armstrong, Galveston.

### Apple Meringue.

Stew six apples, and, while hot, put in a piece of butter the size of an egg. When cold add a cup of cracker crumbs, the yelks of three eggs, one cup of sweet milk, and sugar to taste. Bake in a large plate, with an under crust. When done, beat the whites of the eggs with a cup of sugar to a stiff froth, pour on top the pie and brown. Mrs. J. R. Hutchison.

### Irish Potato Pie.

Boil three or four potatoes until done, then peel and rub through a colander to one cup of sugar, one cup of milk, one tablespoonful of butter and three eggs beaten light. Mix all together, flavor to suit the taste. Bake with under crust.

Mrs. Geo. Bastian.

### Transparent Pie.

Three cups white sugar, three-fourths cup of butter, cream thin, four eggs well beaten, mix. Bake with lower crust. Will make two pies.     Mrs. E. C. Blake.

### Mince Pie Without Meat or Apples.

One and one-half cups chopped bread, one cup molasses, one cup cider, one cup raisins, seeded and chopped, one and one-half cups currants, one and one-half cups brown sugar. Spices to taste.

### Mock Mince Meat.

Six soda crackers rolled fine, two cups cold water, one cup molasses, one cup brown sugar, one cup sour cider, one and one-half cups melted butter, one cup raisins seeded and chopped, one cup currants, two eggs beaten light, one tablespoon cinnamon and allspice mixed, one teaspoon each of nutmeg, cloves, salt and black pepper, one wine-glass brandy.

Mrs. Haynie.

### Prune Meringue.

Take as many prunes as will fill your pudding dish, and stew with just enough sugar and water to cover them. This must be done the evening before you wish to use them. Place the prunes in the dish without the syrup, and make one and a half pounds of sugar into icing and pour it over the prunes until they are well covered, then set the dish in the oven to brown.     Mrs. J. D. Sayers, Bastrop.

### Sweet Potato Pie—No. 2.

One pound of mealy sweet potatoes boiled and pressed through a coarse sieve, one-half cup of butter, one cup of white sugar, one tablespoon of cinnamon, one teaspoon of nutmeg, four eggs, whites and yelks beaten separately, one lemon, juice and rind, one small glass of brandy. Cream, butter and sugar; add the yelks, the spice and lemon, beat the potatoes in by degrees, until all is light, then add the brandy, and stir in the whites. Use no top crust    Mrs. D. C. Smith.

### Cocoanut Pie.

Grate two cocoanuts, stir well together one large tablespoon of butter and one cup of sugar. Beat six eggs until very light, mix them with one pint of rich milk, add this mixture by degrees to the beaten butter and sugar alternately with the cocoanut, stirring well. Bake in a pie-pan or pudding dish.    Mrs. T. W. House.

### Molasses Pie.

Beat the yelks of four eggs, and add one teacup of brown sugar, one-half nutmeg, two tablespoons of butter. Beat thoroughly, stir in one and a half teacups of molasses, add the whites of the eggs.

### Mince Meat—No. 1.

Two and a half pounds tongue, two and a half pounds of lean beef, three and a half pounds beef suet, sixteen good size apples, three pounds raisins, five pounds sugar, three pounds currants, one and a half pounds citron, three quarts sherry, little salt and spices to taste.

### Mince Meat—No. 2.

Two pounds of chopped meat (cooked), two pounds of suet, four pounds of raisins, four pounds of apples, eight oranges with the peel of one, one-half pound citron, chop very fine one ounce each of cinnamon, spice and nutmeg, two pounds of brown sugar, brandy to taste.    Mrs. T. W. House.

### Mince Meat—No. 4.

One pound of finely-chopped roast beef, one-half pound of chopped suet, one-fourth peck of chopped apples, one pound of raisins, one-fourth pound of currants, one-fourth pound of citron, one nutmeg, two tablespoons of cinnamon, juice of two lemons, one pound of sugar, cider and brandy to moisten it.    Mrs. D. C. Smith.

### Mince Meat—No. 3.

Three pounds of beef, three pounds suet, one tablespoon salt sprinkled on the suet and beef, six pounds apples, four pounds raisins, two pounds currants, one tablespoon cinnamon, one nutmeg, a little mace, a few cloves, one quart good whisky, one-half gill brandy, one pound brown sugar, one-half pound citron, cut fine. Put down closely in a stone jar; cover with melted suet.
Mrs. Weems.

### Mince Meat—No. 5.

Three pounds meat (after it is boiled), four pounds suet, three and a half pounds raisins, one and one-half pound currants, one-half pound dried cherries, two nutmegs and mace to taste, four pints white wine, one pint brandy, four pounds brown sugar.

# PUDDINGS.

### Kiss Pudding.

One quart of milk, four tablespoonfuls of corn starch, mixed with a little cold milk, five eggs. Beat the yelks of the eggs with one cup of sugar and the corn starch, put in the milk and let it boil until it thickens, stirring all the time. Beat the whites; add a cup of sugar, flavor and spread over the pudding and brown in the oven.    Mrs. E. R. Falls.

### Chocolate Pudding—No. 1.

Two cups of bread crumbs, three ounces of chocolate, five eggs, taking out three whites, one quart of milk, two cups of sugar, one tablespoonful of butter. Grate the chocolate. Scald the milk and pour one-half over the bread crumbs, and the other half over the chocolate, and let stand until cold. Beat the yelks, and mix butter and sugar with them, then mix all together. Butter a pudding dish, put in the batter, and bake as bread pudding. When done, have a meringue made of the three whites of the eggs beaten stiff, add three tablespoons of sugar, spread over the pudding and brown slightly in the oven.

### Chocolate Pudding—No 2.

One-fourth pound chocolate, grated, three soda crackers, rolled fine, yelks of six eggs stirred with quarter of a pound of sugar, one teaspoon of butter, grated rind of one lemon, whites of the eggs well-beaten. Boil one hour in a close form.

### Chocolate Pudding—No. 3.

Boil three ounces chocolate in one quart of milk. When cold, add the yelks of five eggs, well beaten, with one cup of sugar. Bake twenty-five minutes. Beat the whites of the five eggs stiff, add a little powdered sugar, and when the pudding is done, spread the meringue over the top and return to the oven and slightly brown. Serve cold. Fewer eggs may be used by dispensing with the meringue, and using the whites in the pudding.

### Chocolate Pudding—No. 4.

Melt two ounces butter, mix in two ounces flour, simmer to a soft paste in half a pint of sweet milk, sweeten with two ounces of sugar, and flavor with two ounces of chocolate. When cool, stir in four eggs, yelks well beaten, and whites beat to a stiff froth. Put into a buttered mold immediately, put the mold in a pan half full of hot water, set in the oven and bake one hour. Serve with sauce.

### Chocolate Pudding—No. 5.

Let one pint of milk boil, add half a cup of sugar, three tablespoons of grated chocolate and one large spoonful of corn starch. Boil until thick. Let it cool and serve with sauce.

Mrs. C. W. Hurd.

### Cottage Pudding—No. 1.

Three tablespoons of melted butter, one cup white sugar, two eggs, one pint flour, with two teaspoons yeast powder mixed in dry, one cup sweet milk. Serve with sauce.

Mrs. W. A. S. Haynie.

### Cottage Pudding—No. 2.

Two cups flour, one cup sugar, one cup milk, two tablespoons of butter, one teaspoon cream of tartar, and one egg; beat all together, then add one teaspoon soda. Bake half an hour in moderate oven. Serve with following sauce: White of one egg thickened with sugar, a little butter, beat to a froth, then add a cup of boiling water, stirring all the time, wine, nutmeg, and two tablespoons of milk. Use in the pudding the yelk of egg left from the sauce.

### Chocolate Pudding—No. 6.

Boil one quart of milk; while it is boiling, stir in three and one-half ounces of sweet chocolate, remove from the fire, and while cooling beat seven eggs, leaving out the whites, and stir in the milk, add one tablespoon of butter, make very sweet and flavor with four teaspoons of vanilla, and bake as custard pudding. After it is cold, beat the whites of eggs, with sugar, and frost the pudding. Brown in the oven and serve cold.

Miss Forman, Cynthiana, Ky.

### Snow Pudding—No. 1.

One-half box gelatine, one-half pint cold water, let it soak half an hour, add one-half pint boiling water. When cold, add whites of three eggs, two cups sugar and juice of three lemons. Beat all one-half hour or more. Set away in a mold. Make a boiled custard of the yelks, one and a half pints milk, sugar to taste. Serve the solid part floating in the custard. Miss Forman, Cynthiana, Ky.

### Snow Pudding, No. 2.

Dissolve one box of Coxe's Gelatine in one pint of cold water, let it stand twenty minutes, then pour over it one pint of boiling water, which will dissolve the gelatine, then sweeten very sweet, and add juice of three lemons and break in it the whites of three eggs, take in the cool air and whip with an egg beater until it becomes white jelly. Pour immediately into a mold. Serve with boiled custard.

### Plain Pudding.

One pint milk, three eggs, four tablespoons of flour, one tablespoon of butter, put chopped apples or peaches in the batter and bake. Eat with sauce. Mrs. Haynie.

### A Nice Plain Plum Pudding.

One cup raisins, one cup currants, one-half cup citron, one cup milk, one cup flour, one-half cup sugar, three eggs, one cup rolled cracker, spices to taste. Boil two hours. Eat with hard sauce flavored with brandy.

### Boston Pudding.

Five eggs, four cups flour, two cups sugar, one cup butter, one cup buttermilk, one teaspoon soda, one-half cup brandy.

### Plum Pudding—No. 1.

One pound of raisins, rind and juice of one large lemon. Dredge the raisins with a half pound of currants, half pound of citron, five or six spoons of sugar, half a pound of suet, six eggs, beaten separately, one pint of milk poured in at the last. Scald and flour the bag, and put in boiling water. Boil five hours, and serve with wine sauce.

### SAUCE FOR ABOVE.

Stir to a cream, six tablespoons of loaf sugar and a half pound of butter, then add one egg, one wine-glass of wine, one nutmeg. Mix well together, and set it over the fire to boil.

Mrs. G. A. McDonell.

### Corn Pudding.

To six ears of corn, cut and scraped, use two eggs, whites and yelks beaten separately, one tablespoon of butter, one teaspoon of yeast powder, one-half a cup of milk. Bake in a quick oven.

### Delmonico Pudding.

Yelks of six eggs, six tablespoons of sugar, three of cornstarch, beat all together, boil one quart of milk and stir it into the yelk, sugar and milk, like boiled custard. Set on the fire and let it boil until it becomes thick like custard, stirring constantly, then pour it into a custard bowl and bake until firm. Beat the whites to a stiff froth, add three tablespoons of white sugar, spread over the top of the pudding and bake a light brown. Serve either hot or cold.

### Custard Pudding.

Yelks of twelve eggs, one pound sugar, one-half pound butter; flavor with lemon. Cover a deep dish with puff paste, lay slices of citron over it, and fill with the batter.

Mrs. G. A. McDonell.

### Poor Man's Pudding.

One pint milk, four eggs, two teaspoons of yeast powder, flour enough for a thin batter.

### Sallie Mason Pudding.

To six eggs, take a quart of milk, and to each egg one heaping spoonful of flour. Beat the yelks, and stir the flour in thoroughly, so as not to have it in lumps; pour in the milk. Have ready the whites, well beaten, and stir them in last; have your skillet or pan you intend baking it in hot and greased, so when you pour in the batter it will fry a little at the bottom; place in the stove and bake a short time. Can be eaten with sauce.

### Corn Starch Pudding—No. 1.

One tablespoon of butter, one and one-half quarts of milk, two cups sugar, six eggs, six spoons corn starch. Beat the yelks and sugar together, and stir in the milk while boiling. Beat the whites to a stiff froth, add more sugar, and spread over the top. Place in the oven and brown slightly. Flavor with lemon.

### Quaking Pudding—No. 1.

Scald a quart of rich milk; when almost cold, put to it four eggs, well beaten, one and one-half spoonful of flour, a little nutmeg and sugar. Tie it close in a buttered cloth; boil one hour; turn it out carefully. Eat with wine sauce.

Mrs. T. W. House.

### Black Cap Pudding.

Take a pint of new milk, stir into it by degrees three tablespoons of flour, strain and simmer it over the fire until rather thick, add two ounces of butter; let it grow cold, and stir in the yelks of four eggs, well beaten, and one-half pound currants. Put in a well floured cloth, and boil one hour and a half. Serve with sweet sauce. Mrs. T. W. House.

### Sailors' Duff.

Three eggs, one cup milk, enough flour to make a stiff batter, one glass of currants, one plug of citron, cut very thin, two teaspoons of yeast powder, and a little salt. Tie in a bag and boil twenty minutes. Mrs. T. W. House.

### Transparent Pudding.

Beat yelks of eight eggs, and put in a sauce-pan with one-half pound of butter and one-half pound of sugar, add one pint milk and stir until it thickens, then pour in a bowl and cool. Line your plates with rich paste, put in the custard, and bake in a moderate oven. Put the whites over the whole, and let it brown. Mrs. G. A. McDonell.

### Orange Pudding—No. 1.

Cut five or six oranges in small pieces and place in a pudding-dish; pour over them one cup of coffee sugar. Make a boiled custard of one pint of milk, yelks of three eggs, one-half cup of sugar, one large tablespoon of corn starch; pour this over the oranges. Make a meringue of the beaten whites of the eggs, with three tablespoons powdered sugar, and put over the top of the pudding, and brown slightly in the oven.

### Plum Pudding—No. 2.

Two pounds of flour, two and one-half pounds of suet, two pounds of raisins, two pounds of currants, one pound of citron, one pound of sugar, one-half pound of bread crumbs, one-fourth pound of orange peel, one-fourth pound of spices. Mix all together, and dry. When wanted for use, take a quart of the mixture, and add to it five well-beaten eggs and a wineglass of brandy. Place in a pudding-mold and boil four hours. Eat with creamed butter and sugar sauce flavored with brandy.

Mrs. T. W. House.

### Original Pudding.

One egg, one cup of sugar, one cup of milk, two cups of flour, one tablespoon of butter, one teaspoon of soda, two teaspoons of yeast powder. Eat with sauce.

Mrs. J. A. Peebles.

### Cocoanut Pudding.

One quart of milk, one cocoanut, three-fourths pound of sugar, one tablespoon of butter. First boil the cocoanut (grated) in the milk until done, then add the eggs, sugar and butter. Bake in a rich pastry. Mrs. J. A. Peebles.

### Rice Pudding—No. 1.

Boil the rice until very soft, then add one-half cup of butter, two cups of sugar, one cup of raisins, six eggs, three cups of milk. Makes a large pudding.

Sauce for pudding: Cream, together one-half cup of butter, one half cup milk, about three cups of sugar; grate nutmeg on top. This is nice with a cupful of currants or raisins mixed in. Mrs. J. R. Hutchison.

## PUDDINGS.

### A Very Fine Pudding.

One pint of bread crumbs, one quart sweet milk, one cup sugar, four eggs (yelks), the grated rind of a lemon, piece of butter the size of an egg. Bake till done. Take from the oven and spread a layer of acid jelly over the top. Beat the whites of eggs to a froth, add one cup sugar, flavor with lemon, and spread over the whole. Set in the oven and brown slightly.
Mrs. Usher.

### Tapioca and Apple Pudding.

Soak one cup of tapioca two hours on the back part of the stove (one quart of water to a cup of tapioca), butter a pudding dish and cover the bottom with pared and cored apples. Season tapioca with salt and sugar, nutmeg or cinnamon, and pour over the apples. Bake until apples are thoroughly done. Eat with sugar and cream.

### Tapioca Pudding—No. 1.

Soak one cup tapioca in milk or water (enough to cover it) for two hours, beat three eggs with one cup of sugar, and one large tablespoon of butter, mix all together, and then add one cup of milk; flavor with lemon or vanilla.
Mrs. Geo. Bastian.

### Rice Pudding—No. 2.

One cup of rice, sugar and flavoring to taste, one quart of milk, four eggs, one tablespoon butter; mix well in an earthen bowl, and place the bowl in a pan of cold water. Set the whole in the oven to bake. When nearly done, stir in a pint of cold milk.

### Ginger Pudding.

Six eggs, four cups sugar, two cups butter, two spoons of allspice, two spoons of ginger, two spoons of yeast powder, six cups of flour. Beat all thoroughly, and bake. It is as good warmed as when first baked. Serve with hard or liquid sauce.
Mrs. N. A. Milton.

### Buttermilk Pudding—No. 1.

Four eggs, three cups buttermilk, three cups flour, one of butter, one of sugar, one teaspoon of soda. Serve with sauce.

### Yankee Pudding.

Seven eggs, one cup sugar, two cups molasses, one cup butter, one cup cream, two teaspoons of yeast powder, and flour enough to make a thin batter; add ginger to your taste.
Mrs. N. A. Milton.

### Buttermilk Pudding—No. 2.

Three eggs, three cups buttermilk, one and one-half cups sugar, two cups flour, one-half cup butter, one teaspoon soda; flavor with nutmeg. Bake a nice brown and serve with sauce.

### Rice Pudding—No. 3.

Mix together a pint of soft boiled rice, one and one-half pints of milk, and four well beaten eggs, then add one tablespoon of butter and sugar, nutmeg and powdered sugar to the taste. Bake in a moderate oven.

### Delicious Pudding—No. 1.

Bake a common sponge cake in a layer pan. When ready for use, cut in pieces, split and butter, return to the dish; make a custard with four eggs to a quart of milk; flavor to taste; pour over the cake and bake half an hour.

### Plum Pudding—No. 3.

One-half pound flour, one-half pound raisins, one-half pound currants, milk enough to stir easily; add half pound suet, four eggs, teaspoon mace, cinnamon and allspice. Boil two and one-half hours.
Mrs. James Converse.

### Tapioca Pudding—No. 2.

Soak a tumbler of tapioca several hours, then boil, and while boiling add the grated rind of one lemon and juice of two, sweeten to taste. Boil apples and measure a tumblerful, sweeten, flavor with nutmeg; while hot mix thoroughly.

### Bird's Nest Pudding.

Take nine large apples, pare and core them whole, put them in a deep dish, fill the holes from which you extracted the cores with white sugar, pour round them a little water, just enough to keep them from burning, put them into an oven and let them bake half and hour. In the meantime mix one quarter of a tablespoon of corn starch with a quart of milk, one quarter of a pound of sugar. Beat seven eggs very light and stir them gradually into the milk; then take out the dish of apples, which by this time should be half baked, and pour the batter round the apples, put the dish again into the oven and let it bake half an hour. Reserve four of the whites of the eggs from the pudding and beat to a stiff froth, sweeten a little. When the pudding is cool enough to allow the spreading of the whites on top, place again in the oven and let it remain until it gets a light brown. If agreeable, you can put slices of lemon in the core of the apple while baking.

### Corn Starch Pudding—No. 2.

One pint of milk, two eggs, two even tablespoons starch, two tablespoons sugar. Mix eggs, starch and sugar in a little cold milk. When the rest of the milk is boiling, add the mixture and cook two or three minutes. Use the yelks for the pudding. Beat the whites to stiff froth, and sweeten a little; when the pudding is sufficiently cool place them upon it and bake a light brown. Mrs. Converse.

### Bread and Apple Pudding.

Butter a pudding-dish and lay in it alternate layers of bread crumbs and thinly sliced apples. Sprinkle sugar over each layer of apples, with a little nutmeg or cinnamon. Let the top layer be of bread crumbs, over which pour two or three tablespoons of melted butter, and, if the apples are not juicy, a little water. Serve with cream or wine sauce.

### Lemon Pudding.

Four grated lemons, four eggs, bread crumbs to thicken, one cup of suet, one-half cup of milk, sugar to taste. Steam four hours.

### Sponge Cake Pudding.

Six eggs, three cups flour, two cups sugar, one cup water, one and one-half teaspoons baking powder. Serve hot with sauce. Mrs. J. Hill, Bastrop.

### French Pudding.

One quart sweet milk, yelks of four eggs, four tablespoons

of sugar, two of corn starch. Put in a pudding-dish and cook until it thickens a little more than boiled custard, stirring all the time; then beat the whites with a cup of white sugar, spread over the pudding and brown lightly.

Miss Forman, Cynthiana, Ky.

### Carrot Pudding.

Two cups grated carrots, one cup raisins (stoned), one cup currants, two cups flour, one and one-half cups sugar, two-thirds cup suet, spices to suit the taste. Mix all together, and put in a bag. Boil two hours. Eat with sauce.

### Molasses Pudding.

One cup of molasses, one cup of sugar, one cup of butter or lard, one cup of milk, three eggs, four cups of flour. Beat all together, add one teaspoon of soda or yeast powder. Bake in a deep pan, and eat hot with butter and sugar sauce.

Mrs. N. A. Milton.

### Delicious Pudding—No. 2.

Beat the yelks of six eggs very light, stir in alternately three tablespoons of flour and a pint of milk, one tablespoon of melted butter, with one-half teaspoon of salt, then stir in the whites of the eggs, beaten to a stiff froth. Butter the baking dish or cups, fill them a little more than half full and bake quickly. Eat with wine sauce. Make the pudding half an hour before dinner, as it must be eaten as it is baked. ? ? ?

Mrs. Haynie.

### Plum Pudding—No. 4.

One pound raisins, one pound currants, one-fourth pound butter, one pound flour or grated bread crumbs, eight eggs, one pound sugar, one glass brandy, one-half pint milk, one glass wine, two nutmegs, spice to taste, grated rind of orange or lemon, salt spoon of salt. This pudding requires six hours to boil. Serve with rich sauce.

Mrs. T. C. Armstrong, Galveston.

### Chericoke Pudding.

One quart flour, one light pound butter, three-fourths pound raisins, three-fourths pound preserved cherries, six eggs beaten separately, cream butter and flour, then add cherries and raisins, and lastly the eggs. All the ingredients should be mixed carefully before putting in the eggs. Mix up all soon after breakfast and boil, like any other boiled pudding.

Mrs. E. D. Junkin.

### Apple Tapioca Pudding.

For a dish holding two quarts, take a cup of tapioca and put in a pan with cold water; let it heat and cook gradually, adding (if necessary) hot water and a little salt. In the meantime pare apples enough to fill the dish, core them, and fill holes with sugar and a little nutmeg. Put a little water in the dish and partially bake them, then take the dish from the oven and pour the tapioca over the apples, return it to the oven and bake till the apples are soft. Eat with sugar and cream. Remove from the oven half hour before serving.

### Orange Pudding—No. 2.

Take three sweet oranges, peel and cut in small slices, cover with one-half cup white sugar, and let stand until sugar is dissolved; take then one quart milk, place on the stove and let it come to a boil, beat two eggs, two tablespoonfuls of corn starch and one cup sugar together; add just milk enough to wet it, and then pour into the boiling milk, stirring all the time, until it boils, then put it on the oranges, and stir together until it is perfectly smooth. It looks nicer if you leave out whites of the egg and make meringue for the top. This will bake in a few minutes, and must be eaten cold.

Mrs. L. M. Noble.

### Webster Pudding.

One-half cup molasses, one-half cup sweet milk, one-fourth cup brandy or wine or the juice of two lemons, one-fourth cup melted butter, one-half teaspoon soda dissolved in a little milk, one-half teaspoon cinnamon, one-half teaspoon cloves, one-fourth teaspoon nutmeg, one-half pound raisins or currants, one-fourth teaspoon salt. Dust a pudding-bag with flour, and pour pudding in and steam three hours.

Sauce for same:—Cream two cups sugar and one of butter, and mix with two eggs well beaten, one pint of boiling water one-fourth pint wine, or lemon juice. Set on stove to boil; while boiling, stir in butter, sugar and egg; remove from the fire as soon as melted; flavor with nutmeg or cinnamon.

Mrs. L. C. Noble.

### Cheap Currant Pudding.

Three eggs, beaten separately, three tablespoons of sugar, a small tablespoonful of butter, a saucer of currants, a tumbler of bread crumbs, a tablespoonful of sifted flour, three tumblerfuls of sweet milk, a wine-glass of wine. Boil one hour and a half. To be served with sauce.

### Quaking Pudding—No. 2.

One quart of milk, nine eggs, nine tablespoons of flour, half a teaspoon of salt. Boil two hours. Serve with sauce.

### Apple Pudding.

Eight eggs, leaving out the whites of four, three-fourths pound butter, three-fourths pound brown sugar, the grated crumbs of two rolls, six apples, stewed dry and seasoned with lemon. Cream the butter and sugar together, and add the eggs, beaten very light, the bread crumbs, a teacup of milk and lastly the stewed apples. Put in a buttered tin or dish and bake an hour. Make a meringue of the four whites and four tablespoonfuls of powdered sugar. Spread on the pudding, when done, and brown slightly.

### Excellent Sauce for Pudding.

One-fourth cup butter, one cup sugar, one egg, one wine-glass wine or brandy, one teaspoon flour, one cup boiling water.

Mrs. Vincent.

### Queen of Pudding.

One pint bread crumbs to a quart of milk, one cup of sugar, the yelks of three eggs beaten light, grated rind of a lemon, piece of butter size of an egg, cup of stoned raisins. Bake until done, but not watery. Beat the whites of the eggs to a stiff froth, and stir in a teacup of white sugar, spread over the pudding a layer of jelly, pour over the pudding the whites of the eggs, replace in the oven to bake slightly. This is to be eaten with sauce.

Mrs. L. M. Noble.

## Puddings.

### Estelle Pudding.

Three eggs, two and one-half tablespoon of sugar, two tablespoons of butter, three-fourths cup of sweet milk, one cup of raisins, flour to the consistency of the cake. Steam thirty-five minutes; eat with sauce.

Mrs. James Bailey.

### Lemon Roll.

Two lemons, grate, mix juice and grated rind, roll dough very thin, spread over it the lemon, sweetened with one-half cup of sugar; roll whole up together, put in pan to bake, with sugar, butter, and hot water enough to make a sauce.

Mrs. E. H. Vincent.

### Brown Bettie.

One-third bread, two-thirds apples, two cups brown sugar, one-half cup butter, two teaspoons cinnamon, a little nutmeg; crumb the bread and chop the apples, mix them together, then mix *thoroughly* the sugar, butter and spices, and spread this mixture over the apples and bread. Bake very brown. Serve with sauce made as follows: One teaspoon of butter, one-half cup of brown sugar, one pint of boiling water, one teaspoon of flour, vanilla or wine to flavor it.

### Pudding Sauce.

Four tablespoonfuls sugar, two of butter, one of flour; beat to a cream, add the white of an egg, beaten to a froth, pour into the whole a gill of boiling water, stirring very fast; flavor to taste. The juice of a lemon is very nice.

### German Sauce.

One-half pound butter, eight tablespoons sugar, one cup wine, one-half cup water, one egg or a teaspoon of corn starch mixed in a little water; cream the butter and sugar together, then mix in the other ingredients, and let all come to a boil.

### Wine Sauce for Puddings.

Stir together one teacup of butter, two of sugar and an even tablespoonful of flour. Put these in a stew-pan and stir in it half a tumblerful of boiling water. Let it simmer a minute or two, pour in half a tumbler of wine and grated nutmeg. If preferred, use less water and more wine.

PUDDINGS. 115

### Confederate Sauce for Cake.

Two cups of sugar, one tablespoon of butter, yelk of one egg, beaten well. Mix well, and pour in one-fourth of a pint of boiling milk; add a glass of wine and season with nutmeg.

### Sauce for Pudding.

One pint milk, with as much sugar as can possibly be dissolved by the milk; into which, slice one lemon very thin. No cooking. Prepare just before serving.

### Pudding Sauce.

Mix sugar, butter and a little flour, over which pour water and let it boil. Season with lemon. Beat well one egg, and add while hot.     Mrs. N. A. Milton.

### Eve's Pudding.

If you want a good pudding, mind what you're taught:
Take of eggs six in number, when bought for a groat—
The fruit with which "Eve" her husband did cozen,
Well pared, chopped and cored, at least *half a dozen*;
Six ounces of currants, from the stems you must sort,
Lest you break out your teeth, and spoil all the sport;
Six ounces of bread (let Moll eat the crust),
And crumble the rest as fine as the dust;
Six ounces of sugar wont make it too sweet;
Some salt and a nutmeg will make it complete.
*Three hours* let it boil, without any futter,
But "Adam" wont eat it without wine and butter.

# CAKES.

### Suggestions.

To insure excellent cake, the first essential is, the use of *good* materials. Do not expect a satisfactory result if your flour is second-class, your yeast powder poor, your butter and eggs not sweet and fresh. It is poor economy that induces one to purchase indifferent flour. Always buy a brand you know to be reliable. Yeast powders so flood the land, that it is often a difficult matter to decide which to use. We would recommend, as in every way satisfactory—wholesome as well as efficacious—"*Crawford's Baking Powder*," manufactured in Houston, Texas. A home manufacture, we are able to trace it to its source, and find it all right.

Before beginning cake making, weigh or measure everything required for your cake, that there may be no delays after you begin stirring together the ingredients. Be sure your pans are ready, lined with paper, and well greased. When your batter is beaten until perfectly *light* and *smooth*, pour at once into the *pan*, and put into the oven. *Experience* alone will teach the art of *baking well*. For all loaf cakes, have a moderately heated oven. The thinner the cake, the hotter may be the oven.

### Fruit Cake—No. 1.

One pound butter, two pounds sugar, ten eggs, one pound flour, two pounds raisins seeded, two pounds currants washed and dried, one pound citron finely sliced, one-half cup brandy, one tablespoon each of ground cinnamon, mace and cloves, one teaspoon baking powder. Stir to a cream the butter and sugar, after which add the eggs, well beaten; stir into these the flour and baking powder, and beat well; then, having previously dredged them with flour, add the raisins, currants and citron; stir together well, and add the spices and brandy. Bake in a moderate oven.     Mrs. Geo. Bastian.

### Fruit Cake—No. 2.

One pound powdered sugar, three-fourths pound of butter, one pound of flour, twelve eggs, two pounds of raisins, stoned and part chopped, two pounds currants, carefully washed and dried, one-half pound citron cut in strips, one-fourth of an ounce each of cinnamon, nutmeg and cloves mixed, one wine-glass each of wine and brandy. Cream, butter and sugar, then add yelks of eggs well beaten, part of the flour, the spices and the whites of the eggs, beaten to a stiff froth, then add the wine, remainder of the flour, the brandy, three tablespoons of baking powder. Mix all well together. Bake four hours in a moderate oven.     Mrs. D. C. Smith.

### Fruit Cake—No. 3.

One cup butter, two cups sugar, one cup molasses, one cup sour milk, three pounds raisins, one-half pound citron, three cups flour, three eggs, one ounce cinnamon, one-half ounce cloves, four ounces nutmegs, one teaspoonful soda.

    Mrs. W. A. S. Haynie.

### Rich Fruit Cake.

Two pounds dried and sifted flour, brown it, two pounds of butter, washed free from salt, two pounds of loaf sugar, or coffee A, fifteen eggs, yelks beaten separately, two ounces nutmeg, two ounces mace, two ounces cinnamon, one-half ounce cloves, two pounds currants, two pounds raisins, one pound pecans, chopped very fine, one large glass of brandy, one glass of molasses, one teaspoon of salt. Ice when cold.

    Mrs. M. M. Blake.

### Fruit Cake—No. 5.

Four pounds sugar, three pounds butter, thirty-six eggs, three glasses brandy, three glasses wine, three pounds flour, five pounds raisins stoned and cut, four pounds currants washed and dried, two pounds citron, cut in thin strips, one ounce each of mace and nutmeg, one-half ounce cloves, two teaspoons soda, one gill cream. Beat to a cream the sugar and butter, add the well beaten yelks of the eggs, beating the whole together, then add the spices, well powdered, the brandy, wine and *one pound* of the flour; now add the raisins, currants and citron, having previously dredged them well with flour. Beat the whites of the eggs to a froth, and stir into this two pounds of flour *browned*, add this to the mixture with the soda dissolved in the cream. Bake as soon as the soda is put in. It will require three hours baking. Mrs. E. C. Blake.

### Fruit Cake—No. 4.

Two pounds raisins, one pound of currants, one pound of citron, one pound of sugar, one and one-fourth pounds of flour, twelve eggs, one wine-glass of brandy, one tablespoon each of cinnamon, cloves, allspice and nutmeg. Roll fruit in flour and bake slowly. Mrs. B. D. Orgain, Bastrop, Tex.

### Black Cake.

Two cups molasses, one of sugar, two of butter; mix, set on the fire until the butter melts, take it off and let it cool. Beat five eggs separately, pour the mixture in the yelks, add three cups flour, one of cream, a spoonful of yeast powder, then put in the whites, beat them well, and bake as a pound cake; add about three-fourths of a cup of ginger, spices and cinnamon together. Mrs. Milton.

### White Loaf Cake—No. 1.

One pound each of flour and sugar, three-fourths pound butter, whites of fifteen eggs, one tablespoon yeast powder. Flavor to taste. Stir to a cream the butter and sugar, beat the whites of eggs to a stiff froth, sift together the yeast powder and flour; add to the butter and sugar, alternately, the flour and eggs, beat well and flavor.

### Fruit Cake—No. 6.

One quart flour, one quart sugar (brown), ten eggs beaten separately, two pounds raisins, two pounds currants, three-fourths pound citron, three-fourths pound butter, one-half goblet of brandy or whisky, one tablespoon cinnamon, one teaspoon cloves, one nutmeg, one teaspoon soda, one cup molasses. Bake three hours. Mrs. Vincent.

### Pecan Fruit Cake.

Four pounds raisins, one pound citron, one-half pound pecans, one goblet of wine and brandy mixed, spices—one tablespoon of each kind. Make a pound cake batter, and mix the fruit thoroughly, having previously dredged it well with flour.
Mrs. R. H. White.

### Fruit Cake—No. 7.

One dozen eggs, one pound brown sugar, one pound flour (brown the flour), three-fourths pound butter, two pounds raisins (seeded), two pounds currants (washed and dried), one pound citron cut fine, one pound almonds, one pound pecans, one tablespoon of cinnamon, one tablespoon of cloves, one nutmeg, one wine glass of brandy. Put the fruit in a pan, and rub flour on it; mix the batter; afterwards add the fruit, and bake about two hours.
Miss Julia Crow, Austin.

### Gold Cake.

One pound each of flour and sugar, three-fourths pound butter, six eggs, one-half cup milk, one tablespoon yeast powder. Flavor to taste.

Directions same as preceding.

### White Loaf—No. 2.

One cup butter, two cups sugar, three and one-half cups flour, whites of eight eggs, two teaspoons yeast powder. Flavor with vanilla.

### Yellow Loaf Cake.

Three-fourths cup butter, two cups sugar, three and one-half cups flour, one cup milk, two teaspoons yeast powder, yelks of eight eggs. Flavor with lemon or vanilla.

### White Loaf Cake—No. 3.

One cup butter, two cups sugar, one cup corn starch, two cups flour, one cup milk or water, whites of ten eggs, one teaspoon yeast powder. Flavor to taste.
Mrs. E. H. Vincent, Houston.

### Silver Cake—Excellent.

Whites of sixteen eggs, four cups sugar, six cups flour, one and one-half cups butter, two cups of thick cream, or one can of condensed milk (if the milk is used, take one cup *less* of sugar), four teaspoons of yeast powder, essence of lemon to taste. Put half the yeast powder into the flour, the other half into a cup of cream or milk. Stir together the butter, sugar, and half the flour, then one cup of cream and the whites of the eggs, after which stir in the remainder of the flour, and, lastly, the cup of cream containing the yeast powder.

Mrs. G. A. McDonell.

### White Loaf Cake—No. 4.

Three-fourths pound butter, one pound sugar, one pound flour, whites of sixteen eggs, one teaspoon yeast powder. Flavor with lemon or vanilla.

Miss L. Hutchison, Houston.

### White Loaf Cake—No. 5.

One cup of butter, three cups powdered sugar, whites of twelve eggs, one-half cup of milk, four and one-half cups of flour, one teaspoon yeast powder. Cream, butter and sugar, add eggs, beaten to a stiff froth, then milk and flour.

Mrs. G. A. Gibbons.

### White Loaf Cake—No. 6.

Whites of fourteen eggs, one pound sugar, three-fourths pound flour, one-half pound butter, two teaspoons of yeast powder. Mrs. Wilson.

### White Cake Without Eggs.

Three pounds of sugar, one and one-half pounds of butter, one quart of butter milk, one and one-half teaspoons of ammonia, four and one-half pounds of flour. Bake in jelly-pans lined with greased paper. Mrs. Weems.

### Mountain Cake—No. 1.

One pound flour, one pound sugar, six eggs, one cup butter, one cup butter milk, one teaspoon soda, one teaspoon essence lemon. Bake slowly. Emma Hubbard, Bastrop.

### Angel Cake.

The whites of ten eggs, one cup of sifted flour, one teaspoon of cream of tartar, one teaspoon of soda. Sift the flour, cream of tartar and soda together four times, and beat the whites to a stiff froth, and then beat in one half cup of white sugar, and one teaspoon of vanilla, add the flour, and beat lightly, but thoroughly. Bake until done.

### Angels' Food—No. 1.

Beat the whites of eleven eggs to a stiff froth, take one and a half tumblerfuls of powdered sugar, one tumblerful of flour and one teaspoonful of pure cream tartar. Sift well together, and mix with the eggs, flavor, and bake forty minutes in a moderate oven. Turn the pan upside down to cool. The pan must not be greased.

Miss Julia Crow, Austin.

### Angels' Food—No. 2.

The whites of ten eggs, one goblet of sugar, one goblet of flour, two teaspoons of cream tartar. Bake in a nice pan without greasing. Mrs. Weems.

### Angels' Food—No. 3.

One cup of sifted flour, one-half cup of pulverized sugar, one teaspoon cream tartar, whites of eleven eggs. Mix flour, sugar and cream tartar together, and sift five times. Beat the whites to a stiff froth, and sift in by degrees the flour, etc.; mix well. Put into a perfectly clean, *dry* tin, and bake fifty minutes without opening the stove. The oven should not be too hot while baking; a moderate heat best.

Mrs. Robt. Wilson.

### Snow Cake—No. 1.

One-half pound butter, one-half pound sifted white sugar, one-half pound arrowroot, one-half pound flour, whites of six eggs, flavor to taste. Beat the butter to a cream, then add arrowroot, flour and sugar gradually, beating all the while. Beat the eggs to a stiff froth, and add to the mixture.

Mrs. Jas. Converse, Houston.

### Angels' Food—No. 4.

Beat whites of eleven eggs to a stiff froth, sift into them—little at a time—one and one-half tumblers powdered sugar, mix carefully and lightly, then sift one tumbler of flour four times, add level teaspoon cream tartar to the flour, and then

CAKES.

sift into the eggs and sugar a little at a time, mixing very lightly. When all the flour is used, add teaspoon vanilla. Do not butter or line cake mold; a new tin mold is the best. Bake in moderate oven about an hour. Do not open stove for fifteen minutes after putting in. Test with a straw. If the cake is ready to be taken from the oven, it (the straw) will come out clean. Let it cool gradually. When cool, loosen from the sides with a sharp knife, then turn it out.

Mrs. G. H. Bringhurst, Houston, Tex.

### Snow Cake—No. 2.

One and one-half cups granulated sugar, one cup of flour, one teaspoon yeast powder, whites of eight eggs beaten to a stiff froth; flavor with lemon.

Mrs. O. H. Hutchison, Houston.

### White Sponge Cake.

One cup powdered sugar, one-half cup flour, one-half cup corn starch, one teaspoonful of baking powder. Run all through the sieve together, add the whites of eight eggs beaten to a froth, mix thoroughly, flavor with vanilla. Bake in square tins.

Mrs. O. H. Hutchison.

### Sponge Cake—No. 1.

Twelve eggs, the weight of six eggs in flour, the weight of ten eggs in sugar. Beat eggs very light, stir in the flour, flavor to the taste, and bake in a quick oven.

Mrs. B. D. Orgain, Bastrop.

### Sponge Cake—No. 2.

One pint powdered sugar, ten eggs, juice and rind of one lemon, one pint flour. Beat the yelks of the eggs thoroughly with the sugar, the whites beaten perfectly stiff, add the flour last, and stir in lightly with a fork. Bake in a quick oven.

Mrs. T. C. Armstrong, Galveston.

### Sponge Cake—No. 3.

One pound sugar, one-half pound flour, twelve eggs, rind and juice of two lemons, one teaspoonful yeast powder. Beat yelks and sugar together; put the whites in after putting in flour.

Mrs. James Converse.

### Sponge Cake—No. 4.

Eleven eggs, three-fourths pound flour, one pound of sugar, grated rind and juice of one large lemon. Beat the sugar and yelks of eggs together, until they are very light, then add the lemon; and lastly, the whites of eggs, beaten stiff, with the flour.

This is an excellent receipt for picnics, festivals, etc.

Mrs. E. C. Atkinson.

### Sponge Cake Roll.

Six eggs, two cups sugar, two cups flour, two tablespoonfuls milk, one teaspoonful yeast powder. Beat well together, turn into square jelly tins, and bake in a quick oven. When done, turn out on a molding board and spread quickly with jelly, roll carefully, and wrap each roll in a clean napkin.

Miss Louisa Hutchison.

### Good Sponge Cake.

Two cups sugar, two cups flour, one cup water, four eggs beaten separately, one teaspoonful yeast powder, flavor to the taste.

Mrs. E. H. Vincent.

### Sponge Cake—No. 5.

Two cups sugar, two cups flour, eight eggs, two teaspoonfuls yeast powder.

Mrs. McDowell, Bastrop.

### Sponge Cake—No. 6.

Three eggs, one cup sugar, one cup flour, two tablespoons of milk or water, two small teaspoons of yeast powder. Flavor with lemon.

Mrs. A. A. Adey.

### Cheap Sponge Cake.

One cup powdered sugar, four eggs, one teaspoonful of yeast powder, mixed well with one cup of flour, one and one-half tablespoons of water. Beat the eggs and sugar thoroughly together, flavor with lemon, and bake twenty minutes.

Miss Julia Crow, Austin.

### Sponge Cake—No. 7.

Beat six eggs, yelks and whites together *two minutes*, add three cups of sugar and beat *five minutes*, two cups of flour and beat *two minutes*, one cup of cold water and beat one minute; add two more cups of flour and three teaspoons of yeast powder, and beat one minute. Flavor to taste. Bake in an ordinary bread-pan one hour. This never fails. While baking, do not move more than can possibly be avoided.

Mrs. L. C. Noble.

### Lady Fingers.

Take sponge cake batter, form an oval shape on sheets of white paper slightly damp. Make them three inches long, of uniform size. When done, remove carefully from the paper, cover the under side of one with jelly, lay on this another cake, fitting them neatly. They may be cemented together with icing instead of jelly.

Sponge cake is excellent made of half corn starch.

### Water Sponge Cake.

Seven eggs, one pound sugar, ten ounces flour, one-half goblet of water, one-half teaspoonful of salt. Dissolve half of the sugar in the water, beat the remaining sugar with yelks of the eggs, beat the whites to a stiff froth, and add with the flour as in ordinary sponge cake.

### Delicate Cake.

One cup of butter, one cup of sweet milk, two cups of flour, one cup of corn starch, whites of seven eggs, one teaspoon cream tartar, one teaspoon soda.

Miss Agnes L. Dwight, Chicago.

### Delicate Cake for Tea.

Beat the yelks and whites of two eggs separately; to the yelks add two coffee cups of sugar and two cups of sweet milk, four tablespoons of butter, creamed, next add the beaten whites of eggs, lastly, four cups of flour, with one teaspoon of soda, two of cream tartar, sifted in the flour. Bake in shallow pans.

Mrs. Haynie.

### Pecan Cake.

One cup butter, three cups sugar, four cups flour, one cup milk, six eggs, two teaspoons of yeast powder, one and one-half pints of pecans, chopped finely; add the pecans last.

Mrs. E. C. Atkinson.

### Nun's Puffs.

Boil one pint of milk with half pound of butter. Stir this into three-fourths of a pound of flour, and let it cool; add nine eggs, yelks and whites beaten separately, whites added last, fill cups or tins half full and bake. When done, sprinkle with white sugar while hot. Very nice for tea.

Mrs. Haynie.

### Apple Cake.

Take two cups dried apples, stew in water just enough to cut easily, chop about as fine as raisins. Boil them in two cups of molasses until preserved through, drain off the molasses for the cake, then add two eggs, one cup of butter, one cup of sour milk, two teaspoons yeast powder, four cups flour, spices of all kinds, add apples last.

Mrs. Haynie.

### Feather Cake.

Half cup of butter, three of flour, two of sugar, one of milk, three eggs, a little grated lemon, two teaspoons baking powder.

### Corn Starch Cake—No. 1.

One cup butter, two cups sugar, one cup corn starch dissolved in a cup of sweet milk, two cups flour, whites of eight eggs. Always take less than a cup of Goshen butter. After you have the butter and sugar very light, stir the corn starch and put with the butter and sugar, then beat your whites, and put in first some flour, then whites, and so on, until you have used all; beat well; two teaspoons yeast powder. For the yelks, take less than a cup of butter, two cups sugar, one cup milk, three and one-half cups flour, yeast powder.

### Pound Cake—No. 1.

One pound butter, one pound sugar, one pound flour, ten eggs, whites and yelks beaten separately, one teaspoonful yeast powder, flavor to suit the taste.

Lou Hutchison.

### Seed Cake.

Beat one pound of butter to a cream, dredge into it one pound of flour (sifted); when the two are well mixed, add three-fourths pound of powdered loaf sugar, pounded mace and grated nutmeg to the taste, and three-fourths of an ounce of caraway seed. Stir well until all the ingredients are well mixed. Beat up six eggs with a wine-glass of pale brandy, add to the cake mixture, and continue stirring it for a quarter of an hour. Bake in buttered tins.

### Pork Cake.

One teacup of raw salt pork, chopped fine, one cup of sugar, one cup of molasses, one cup of raisins, one cup sweet milk, one egg, all kinds of spice, one cup of currants, one teaspoon of soda, flour enough to make a little thicker than common cake.

### White Fruit, or Cocoanut Cake.

Twelve eggs, one pound of butter, one pound of flour, one cocoanut, two pounds of almonds in hull—they should be blanched and cut in half—one pound of citron; leave out this, if you wish, though it is nicer with the citron. Some put two pounds of cocoanut. Put two teaspoons of yeast powder in every cake.

### Hickorynut Cake.

One cup of nuts (chopped fine), one-half cup of sugar (white), one cup of sweet cream; mix and spread as jelly.

Mrs. Weems.

### Soft Ginger Cake.

One cup sugar, one cup butter, one cup milk four teaspoons pulverized ginger, four eggs, four cups flour, one cup of syrup warmed to milk heat, one teaspoon soda, cream butter and sugar. Bake in quick oven.

### Superior Ginger Cake.

Two eggs, one-half cup sour milk, one-half quart molasses, one-half cup sugar, one-half cup butter, one-half cup lard, ginger to taste, one tablespoon soda mixed in molasses, eggs and sugar beaten together, butter worked in the flour; handle as *little* as *possible*. The dough should be soft and baked in a quick oven.

Mrs. G. A. McDonell.

### Ginger Cake.

One cup of butter, cup of brown sugar, one cup of molasses,

two eggs, one half cup of water, with teaspoon of soda, four cups of flour, two teaspoons of ginger.

Mrs. J. R. Hutchison.

### Boston Ginger Bread.

One cup of sugar, one cup of molasses, not syrup, one-half cup of butter, one-half cup of milk, one cup of raisins or currants, one teaspoon of yeast powder, cloves to taste, flour to make as stiff as cup cake.

Mrs. D. C. Smith.

### Ginger Bread.

One cup brown sugar, one cup of syrup, one cup butter, three eggs, two thirds cup of sweet milk, two teaspoons yeast powder, two teaspoons each of ginger, cinnamon cloves and allspice, one-half nutmeg.

### Hard Ginger Bread.

Two pints molasses, one cup milk, four eggs, three tablespoons ginger, flour enough to make a dough. Leave out one of the whites of the eggs to glaze the cake before baking. Cut in squares and bake.

Mrs. Vincent.

### Pound Cake—No. 2.

One pound butter, one pound flour, one pound sugar, ten eggs, one nutmeg, one gill brandy.

Mrs. J. R. Morris.

### Tea Cake.

One cup of butter, two cups of sugar, four eggs, two cups of milk, one teaspoonful of yeast powder, flour sufficient to roll thin. Flavor with lemon or vanilla. Sift white sugar over when rolled for cutting. Bake in a quick oven.

Miss Lou Hutchison.

### Cup Cake—No. 1.

One cup butter, two cups sugar, three cups flour, one teaspoon yeast powder, five eggs, beaten thoroughly, one-half cup milk.

Mrs. O. H. Hutchison.

### Cup Cake—No. 2.

One cup of butter, two and one half cups sugar, five eggs, one cup of milk, four cups of flour, one teaspoon of baking powder. Flavor with lemon.

Mrs. Geo. Bastian.

### A Good Cake.

One cup sweet milk, one cup butter, three cups sugar, five cups of flour, two teaspoons baking powder.

### Corn Starch Cake—No. 2.

Take the whites of eight eggs, one-fourth pound each of corn starch, flour and butter, one-half pound of sugar, one teaspoonful cream tartar, one-half teaspoonful of soda. Flavor with almond to suit the taste. L. BARRET.

### Cookies—No. 1.

Two cups of sugar, one cup of sweet milk, one cup of butter, two teaspoons of baking powder, flour enough to roll. Flavor with vanilla, lemon, nutmeg, or carraway seed. Very nice. MRS. J. L. CUNNINGHAM.

### Cookies—No. 2.

One cup of white sugar, one-half cup of butter, one egg, two tablespoons sweet milk, two teaspoons of baking powder, add sufficient flour to roll thin. MRS. J. D. SAYERS.

### Jumbles.

One pound of white sugar, three-fourths pound of butter, five eggs, leaving out the yelks of two, nearly two pounds of flour. Spice to taste.

### Cookies Without Eggs.

One cup of butter, two and one-fourth cups of brown sugar, one cup of sweet milk, two teaspoons yeast powder, flour enough to make a soft dough, a little grated nutmeg.

### Soda Cake.

Three eggs, three cups sugar, one cup of butter, one cup of cream, one teaspoon of soda, one-half nutmeg grated, flour enough to roll thin; cut into tea cakes. Roll sugar on top of dough before cutting.

### Ginger Cookies.

Two and one-half cups molasses, one cup sugar, one-half cup butter, one-half cup lard, four teaspoonfuls ginger, two teaspoonfuls soda dissolved in a little warm water. Stir in flour gradually, making a paste as soft as can be easily rolled. MRS. T. C. ARMSTRONG, Galveston, Tex.

CAKES.

### Ginger Crackers—No. 1.

Two and one-half cups molasses, one cup sugar, one and one-half cups butter, one-fourth cup ginger, two small teaspoons soda, two small teaspoons cinnamon. Warm all the ingredients together, except the flour, of which use enough to make a soft dough.

### Snappish Ginger Snaps.

Into a teacup put one teaspoon of soda, one of ginger, six of lard and four of water. Fill the cup with molasses and use flour enough to roll thin.  Mrs. J. L. Cunningham.

### Ginger Snaps.

One pint molasses, one teacup butter, two tablespoonfuls powdered ginger, one teaspoonful soda. Boil together the molasses and butter, let it stand till cool, add the ginger and soda, and flour enough to roll it well. Roll out quite thin and bake quickly.  Mrs. R. E. C. Wilson.

### Ginger Crackers—No 2.

Five cups molasses, two cups sugar, three cups butter, three-fourths cup ginger, four teaspoons of soda, four teaspoons of cinnamon. Warm all the ingredients together, except the spice, before putting into the flour.

### Cocoanut Tea Cake.

One pound of sugar, one-half pound of butter, six eggs, one tablespoon of yeast powder, one grated cocoanut, flour sufficient to make a soft dough. Roll out and cut into tea cakes, and bake in a moderate oven.  Mrs. G. A. McDonell.

### Crullers—No. 1.

Two cups sugar, three eggs, one cup sweet milk, butter the size of an egg, one-half nutmeg, two teaspoons yeast powder. Roll and cut in small strips and fry in hot lard.

### Crullers—No. 2.

Five eggs, one and one-half teacups brown sugar, two tablespoons sweet milk, one teaspoon of butter, one teaspoon of cinnamon, two teaspoons of yeast powder. Have a great deal of hot lard in the spider; use enough flour to make a soft dough. Cut in thick squares and fry.

Miss Julia Crow, Austin.

### Crullers—No. 3.

Four eggs, four tablespoons of butter, four *heaping* tablespoons sugar. Mix soft for rolling.  Mrs. Vincent.

### Crullers—No. 4.

Three eggs, three heaping tablespoons of white sugar, three tablespoons of butter or lard, one-half teaspoon of yeast powder, or one-half teaspoon of soda, and one teaspoon of cream tartar. If lard is used, put in a little salt; cut in shapes and fry in boiling lard.

### Crullers—No. 5.

Three eggs, one cup sugar, one-half cup butter, one cup milk, three teaspoons of yeast powder, one nutmeg, or one teaspoon of cinnamon, lemon juice to taste; flour to stiffen. Roll, cut and fry in hot lard  Mrs. G. A. McDonell.

### Doughnuts.

One quart of flour, two heaping teaspoons of baking powder; mix by sifting. Beat two eggs with two cups of sugar and one cup of milk; flavor with nutmeg; mix all together, reserving a little flour for rolling out. Cut in any shape, and fry in boiling lard.  Mrs. Geo. Bastian.

### Ammonia Jumbles.

Three-fourths of a pound of lard, two pounds of sugar, two eggs, one ounce of carbonate of ammonia dissolved in one and a half pints of warm water; flour enough to roll; mix as jumbles and bake quickly. This recipe is especially recommended for its great excellence.  Mrs. M. E. Davis.

### Wafers.

Two tablespoons of rolled white sugar, the same of butter, one coffeecup of flour, and essence of lemon; add milk enough for a thick batter. Bake in buttered wafer irons, and then strew on white sugar.

### Mountain Cake—No. 2.

One cup of white sugar, one-half cup of butter, one-half cup of sweet milk, three eggs, two cups of flour, two teaspoons yeast powder; add a little fruit, and flavor with lemon.
 Miss Julia Crow, Austin.

### Snow Cake—No. 3.

Whites of eight eggs beaten to a stiff froth, one and one-half cups of granulated sugar, one cup of flour, one teaspoon of yeast powder. a little salt.   Miss Julia Crow, Austin.

### Spice Cake—No. 1.

One pound of flour, one pound of brown sugar, four eggs, one nutmeg, one tablespoon of cinnamon, one ounce of cloves. Roll out in squares and bake.

Miss Julia Crow, Austin.

### Marble Cake—No. 1.

One cup sugar, two large spoonfuls of butter, rubbed together; add one cup sweet milk, one egg well beaten, a pinch of salt; stir two teaspoons baking powder into two cups of flour and add. For the dark part, take one-third mixture and make dark with spices, and lay in the pan in layers with the white.   Mrs. J. L. Cunningham.

### Marble Cake—No. 2.

Dark batter: Two cups brown sugar, two cups molasses, yelks of eight eggs, one and one-half cups butter, five cups flour, one cup of sour cream, one teaspoon of soda, cloves, mace, cinnamon, black pepper, allspice, each one teaspoon. White batter: Whites of eight eggs, two cups sugar, one and one-half cups butter, four cups flour, one cup sweet cream, one teaspoon cream tartar, one half teaspoon soda; pour in pan in alternate white and dark batter.

### Marble Cake—No. 3—Very Nice.

White part: Beat well together one cup white sugar, one-half cup butter, one-half cup sweet milk, whites of three eggs, and two coffeecups of flour, and lastly, add one teaspoonful of cream tartar, one-half teaspoon soda. Dark part: Use one-half cup brown sugar, one-half cup butter, one-half cup sugarhouse molasses, and one-fourth cup of sweet milk or water, one-half nutmeg, one teaspoon cinnamon, one of allspice, one-fourth teaspoon cloves, about half a slice citron cut fine, and a teacup of raisins seeded and chopped, two cups flour and yelks of three eggs; lastly, one teaspoon cream tartar, and half that quantity of soda. Bake as any other cup cake, but let it stay in the stove ten or fifteen minutes longer.

### Spice Cake—No. 2.

One cup brown sugar, one of molasses, one of butter, one of milk, nutmeg, cinnamon and cloves, one teaspoon each, three eggs, two teaspoonfuls of yeast powder, and four small cups of flour.

### Marble Cake—No. 4.

One and one-half cups white sugar, one-half cup butter two and one-half cups flour, whites of six eggs, teaspoonful yeast powder, one and one-half cups milk.

#### DARK BATTER.

One cup brown sugar, one-half cup molasses, one-half cup butter, two and one-half cups flour, yelks of six eggs, teaspoon yeast powder, tablespoon cinnamon, teaspoon each allspice, cloves, and nutmeg.

### Neapolitan Cake—No. 1.

The white batter is made of the whites of nine eggs, one teacup butter, two teacups sugar, three and one-half of flour. one teaspoon yeast powder, teacup sweet milk.

The dark batter is the yelks of nine eggs, one teacup brown sugar, one-half teacup molasses, one-half teacup butter milk, one-half teaspoon soda, two and one-half cups flour, tablespoon cinnamon, teaspoon each allspice, cloves and ginger, one pound raisins, one-half pound currants, one-half pound citron.

Bake the white and dark portions separately, in pans of about an inch and one-half in depth. Arrange in layers, the fruit cake at bottom, with icing between.

Miss Lucy Miller, Ky.

### Neapolitan Cake—No. 2.
#### YELLOW.

Two cups of powdered sugar, one cup of butter, five eggs, beaten well and separately, one-half cup sweet milk, three cups prepared flour, a little grated orange peel.

### PINK AND WHITE.

One pound sugar, one pound prepared flour, one-half pound butter, warmed with the sugar, ten eggs, whites only, beaten stiff Make the batter and divide in two equal portions; leave one white, and flavor with lemon, color the other with cochineal, and flavor with rose.

### BROWN.

Three eggs, beaten light, one cup powdered sugar, one fourth cup butter, creamed with sugar, two tablespoons cream, and one heaping cup prepared flour, two tablespoons of grated chocolate rubbed smooth in the cream before it is beaten in the cake. Bake all in jelly cake tins.

The above quantity should make one dozen cakes—three of each color. If prepared flour cannot be had, use with ordinary flour yeast powder, or soda and cream tartar.

### FILLING.

Two cups of sweet milk, two tablespoons of corn starch, wet with the yelks of eight eggs, two small cups of powdered sugar. Heat the milk, stir in the sugar, corn starch and eggs. Let it boil, stirring steadily until quite thick. Divide this custard into two parts, stir into one part two tablespoons of grated chocolate and a teaspoon of vanilla; into the other, the juice and gaated rind of one orange.

### PINK.

Whites of three eggs, beaten stiff, one heaping cup of powdered sugar. Color with cochineal and flavor with rose.

Arrange the cakes as your fancy dictates. Ice with white frosting, flavored with lemon.    MISS FORMAN, Ky.

## Jenny Lind Cake—No. 1.

One cup of sugar, one-half cup of butter, one half cup of milk, one and one-half cups of flour, whites of two eggs, one-half teaspoonful of soda. one teaspoonful cream tartar. Bake in two tins.

### DARK LAYER.

One cup of brown sugar, one-half cup of butter, one-half cup of milk, yelks of four eggs, one and one-half cups of flour, one-half teaspoonful of soda, one teaspoonful cream tartar, one cup of raisins or currants. Spices to taste. Bake in one tin.

Put the dark between the two white cakes, with icing between each layer.                    Mrs. J. R. PEEBLES.

### Jenny Lind Cake—No. 2.

Three cups of sugar, five cups of flour, four eggs, two cups of sweet milk, two heaping tablespoons of butter, two teaspoons of baking powder. Flavor to taste, and fruit if preferred. Rub butter and sugar to a cream, add the eggs, and beat thoroughly; last of all add the milk and flour alternately until all is smoothly stirred in.

#### CHOCOLATE ICING FOR ABOVE.

Whites of three eggs, two tablespoons sugar, two squares of chocolate, grated. Spread this between the layers.

### Tea Cakes.

Four eggs, two cups of sugar, one cup of butter milk, one cup of butter, one teaspoonful of soda, flour enough to roll thin.

### Imperial Cake.

Whites of nine eggs, one teacup butter, two teacups sugar, three and one-half teacups flour, teaspoon baking powder, a teacup nearly full sweet milk, tablespoon whisky. Bake this as for jelly cake—about three cakes, then a layer of fruit between the cakes.

### Receipt for the fruit.

One pound blanched almonds cut fine, one pound chopped raisins, one pound cut figs, three-fourths pound citron cut fine, one wine-glass whisky. Mix all these well together. Have icing made of the whites of three eggs, one-half pound sugar. When the icing is stirred smooth and glossy, add the fruit, and then put between the layers of cake. Ice on the outside if you choose.                    Mrs. F. W. HENDERSON.

### Ice Cream Cake.

Whites of eight eggs, one cup sweet milk, one cup butter, two cups sugar, two cups flour, one cup corn starch, two teaspoons baking powder, mixed well with the flour. Bake in jelly cake tins.

### ICING FOR ABOVE.

Whites of four eggs, well beaten, four cups of sugar; pour one-half pint boiling water over the sugar, and boil until it ropes on being poured from a spoon; pour the boiling syrup over the beaten eggs, and beat hard until the mixture is cold. Before quite cool, add one teaspoon pulverized citric acid, two teaspoons vanilla. Spread thickly between the cakes.

Mrs. JULIA HILL, Bastrop.

### Dolly Varden Cake.

Eight eggs, four cups sugar, one of butter; beat well, and add six cups of flour, one and one-half cups of milk, four teaspoonfuls of baking powder, or one-half teaspoon of soda and one of cream tartar. Take half of the quantity in another dish and add two cups of raisins cut in halves, two cups currants, one nutmeg, four teaspoons of cinnamon, same of cloves. Bake in layers, and ice between each layer.

Miss FORMAN, Ky.

### Water Melon Cake.

#### WHITE PART.

Two cups white sugar, one cup butter, one cup sweet milk, three and a half cups flour, whites of eight eggs, two teaspoons cream tartar, one teaspoon soda dissolved in a little warm water.

#### RED PART.

One cup red sugar, one-half cup butter, one-third of a cup of sweet milk, two cups flour, whites of four eggs, one teaspoon cream tartar, one-half teaspoon soda, one teacup of raisins.

In filling the cake-pan, put the white around the edges, on the bottom and over the top, making the centre of the red, with raisins sprinkled throughout to represent seed.

Mrs. H. F. HURD.

### Butter Milk Cake.

One cup of butter, two cups of sugar, three cups of flour,

CAKES.

one cup of butter milk, six eggs, one nutmeg, one teaspoon of soda, two teaspoons of cream tartar.

Mrs. J. D. Sayers.

### Washington Cake.

One and one-half cups of sugar and one cup of butter, three eggs and one cup of milk, three cups of flour, and three teaspoons of yeast powder.

### Washington Pie.

Three cups of sugar, four cups of flour, one cup of butter, one and one-half cups of sweet milk, one and one-half teaspoons of soda, three eggs. Flavor with lemon and serve with sauce.

### Lemon Jelly Cake—No. 1.

One cup of butter, one-half cup of milk or water, two cups of sugar, three cups of flour, four eggs, two teaspoons yeast powder.

FILLING FOR THE ABOVE.

One-half cup sugar, two eggs, well beaten, the juice and grated rind of two lemons, two tablespoons of water, two tablespoons of flour. Place it in a kettle of boiling water until it thickens. When cool spread between cakes.

Mrs. Wm. Christian.

### Lemon Cake—No. 1.

One pound of sugar, one-half pound of butter, the grated rind and juice of two lemons, two wine-glasses of currants, one pound of flour, eight eggs, one teaspoon of yeast powder.

Mrs. J. R. Morris.

### Lemon Cake—No. 2.

One cup of butter, three cups of powdered sugar, rubbed to a cream, five eggs, well beaten, one small teaspoon of soda, one cup sweet milk, the juice and grated rind of one lemon, four cups of flour. Stir in as light as possible. Bake in two tin sheets. Is improved by icing. Miss Dwight.

### Lemon Jelly Cake—No. 2.

One-half cup of sugar, one-half cup of butter, beat to a

cream, one-half cup of milk, two and a half cups of flour, three eggs, one teaspoon yeast powder. Bake in sheets.

### JELLY FOR SAME.

One cup of sugar, one egg, grated rind and juice of one lemon, one tablespoon of water, one teaspoon flour. Place the dish in a kettle of boiling water and let it thicken. When cool, spread between cakes.     Miss L. Hutchison.

### Filling for Lemon Cake.

One-half cup of butter, one-half cup of sugar, yelks of three eggs, the juice and rind of two lemons. Beat the eggs well, cream butter and sugar, then mix all; set on the fire, stirring all the while, until it thickens. It will change color, and become lighter as it is done.

### Rolled Jelly Cake—No. 1.

One cup of sugar and two eggs well beaten together, then add two tablespoons of water. Mix one and one-half teaspoons of yeast powder with one and one-half cups of flour; add this to the eggs and sugar. Do not stir much after adding flour. Bake in a dripping-pan in a quick oven. When cool spread with jelly and roll.     Mrs. Wm. Christian.

### Rolled Jelly Cake—No. 2.

Butter your baking-pans first. Mix two teaspoons of yeast powder with one cup of flour. To three well-beaten eggs add one cup of white sugar; then add the flour and stir well, add some milk, stir till well mixed. Bake in long shallow pans. When done turn the cake out immediately bottom side up on a smooth towel. Spread quickly with jelly and roll. Cover with the towel to keep moist. This is nice with wine sauce.

### Coffee Cake—No. 1.

One cup of butter, one cup of sugar, one cup of molasses, one cup of strong coffee, five cups of flour, one pound of raisins, one teaspoonful of soda, one teaspoonful of cinnamon, one teaspoonful of allspice, one-half nutmeg, three eggs. Sift the soda into the molasses.     Miss Agnes Dwight.

### Coffee Cake—No. 2.

One cup of butter, one and one-half cups of sugar, one egg,

one cup of molasses, one cup of cold strong coffee, four cups of flour, one nutmeg, one-half teaspoonful of cloves, one teaspoonful of soda, one-half teaspoonful of cream tartar, one cup raisins.      Mrs. Jas. Converse.

### Orange Cake.

Two cups sugar, one-half cup water, five eggs, leaving out the white of one, two cups flour, one orange, grated rind and juice, one-half teaspoon of soda, and one of cream tartar.

### Cocoanut Cake—No. 1.

Two cups of sugar, one-half cup of butter, one cup of milk, three cups of flour, three eggs, two teaspoons of yeast powder. Bake in jelly cake tins.

### Filling for Cocoanut Cake.

One grated cocoanut. Take three-fourths of it, add whites of three eggs, beaten to a stiff froth and one cup of powdered sugar. Spread this between the layers of cake. Mix with the remainder of cocoanut four tablespoons of powdered sugar and spread thickly over top of the cake.

     Mrs. J. D. Sayers.

### Cocoanut Cake—No. 2.

One pound of flour, one pound of sugar, one-half pound of butter, one grated cocoanut, ten eggs, one teaspoon of soda, two teaspoons of cream tartar, one cup sweet milk. Cream butter and sugar, then add yelks, whites of eggs, and flour, well stirred in with soda and cream tartar, then cocoanut, lastly milk.     Mrs. R. H. White.

### Chocolate Cake—No. 1.

Three cups white sugar, one cup butter, one cup sweet milk three cups flour, one cup corn starch, three teaspoons yeast powder, whites of eight eggs.

Make another batter by the same recipe, only using the yelks of the eggs instead of the whites, and add half a cake of chocolate, grated. Bake in jelly cake tins.

Make a chocolate icing and spread between layers, putting alternate layers of light and dark cake.

     Mrs. Parker, La.

### Coffee Cake—No. 3.

Two cups of sugar, one cup of molasses, one cup of butter, one cup of strong dripped coffee, four eggs, five cups of flour, two teaspoons each of cloves, mace and cinnamon, two teaspoons of soda, dissolved in a little water, one-half pound of chopped raisins. Mrs. T. C. Armstrong.

### Cocoanut Chocolate Cake.

Grate one cocoanut. Make a syrup of two cups of sugar, half cup of butter, creamed, and one cup of water. Let it boil until the consistency of sauce for cake, then put in the cocoanut and let it boil till the cocoanut is done. Grate one cake of chocolate, and add half to the cocoanut. Grate in a little nutmeg. Cook until all is the consistency of thick jam, then take from the fire and let it stand until almost cold. Flavor with vanilla, and spread between cakes.

Make boiled icing, and add the rest of the chocolate, and ice the top and sides of the cake.

Miss E. Baxter, Shreveport.

### Frosting.

White of one egg, sufficient sugar to make icing, one orange, grated rind and juice.

### Chocolate Cake—No. 2.

One cup of butter, two cups of sugar, one cup of milk, four cups of flour, five eggs, two teaspoons of baking powder.

#### CUSTARD FOR THIS.

One pint milk, one cup of sugar, one egg, three tablespoons corn starch or flour, one cake chocolate (grated). Flavor highly with vanilla. Mix the custard and put in a pan, then place the pan into a larger vessel of boiling water, and let it cook until quite thick. Allow to *cool*, but not get *cold*. Spread it between the cakes as you take them from the oven.

Mrs. E. C. Atkinson.

### Chocolate Cake—No. 3.

Two cups sugar, one cup butter, yelks of five eggs, and whites of two, one cup of milk, three and one-half cups of flour, two teaspoons of yeast powder. Bake in jelly cake tins.

### FILLING FOR SAME.

Whites of three eggs, one and one-half cups of sugar, three tablespoons grated chocolate, one teaspoon of vanilla. Beat all together and spread between the cakes.

Miss Lou Hutchison.

### Chocolate Cake—No. 4.

Two cups sugar, one cup butter, three cups flour, five eggs, one cup milk, one teaspoon cream tartar, one-half teaspoon soda. Bake in thin cakes.

Take nearly a cup of grated chocolate, sweeten to taste, add milk enough to moisten. Flavor with vanilla, and spread between cakes.

Mrs. Julia Hill, Bastrop.

### Cream Cake—No. 1.

One cup butter, three cups sugar, five eggs, one cup cream or milk, four and one-half cups of flour, two teaspoons yeast powder. Flavor highly to suit the taste. An excellent cake.

Mrs. E. C. Atkinson.

### Cream Jelly Cake.

Six eggs, two teacups sugar, two teacups flour, six dessert spoons of country butter or three of Goshen. Cream the butter and sugar together, and add the yelks well beaten. Beat the whites to a stiff froth and stir in, with the flour alternately; add one teaspoon of cream tartar, and one-fourth teaspoon of soda, or one teaspoon of yeast powder.

### Cream Jelly for Cake.

One large cup of milk or cream and two teaspoons of sugar. Put it on a quick fire, and when it boils add two teaspoons of corn starch dissolved in a little cold milk. Let it bubble on the fire for a few minutes, and when cold flavor highly with vanilla. Spread between the cakes as any other jelly.

Mrs. James Converse.

### Cream Cake—No. 2.

The weight or nine eggs in sugar, the weight of six in flour. Beat the yelks and whites separately. Bake in two tin sheets. This will make two loaves of two layers each.

Miss Dwight, Chicago, Ill.

## Cakes.

### Cream Puffs—No. 1.

One-half pound butter, three-fourths pound flour, one pint water. Boil butter and water together, and, while boiling, stir in the flour; then let it cool and add ten eggs, the whites beaten separately, pinch of soda, dissolved in a little boiling water. Grease your pans well, drop a small spoonful, leaving space enough for them to rise. Bake about forty-five minutes in a moderate oven.

#### MIXTURE FOR FILLING THE PUFFS.

Two cups sugar, one cup flour, one quart milk, four eggs. Boil the milk, beat eggs, flour and sugar together, and stir into the milk while boiling until the mixture thickens. Flavor with lemon. Let it cool, and fill your cakes.

Mrs. Haynie.

### Cream Puffs—No. 2

Stir into a pint of boiling water three cups (coffee) of flour, one cup of butter (or butter and lard mixed), rubbed smooth. After it is cool, beat in five eggs, one at a time. Bake in small tins, nearly a tablespoon of the stiff batter in each tin, about fifteen minutes. While hot or cool, open at the side and spread in cream, which is a thick custard of two eggs, one cup sugar one pint milk, two tablespoons corn starch, flavored with vanilla.

### Cream Custard Cake.

Four eggs, one cup sugar, well beaten, four tablespoons cold water, one cup flour, two teaspoons yeast powder. Bake in jelly cake tins.

#### FILLING FOR ABOVE.

One cup milk, two tablespoons sugar. Just before boiling, add one and one-half tablespoons flour dissolved in a little milk, and one egg, well beaten. Stir this until it boils. When cool add one tablespoon of vanilla. Spread between the layers of cake.

Miss Julia Crow, Austin.

### Custard Cake—No. 1.

Six eggs, two cups sugar, two cups flour, two tablespoonfuls milk, one teaspoonful yeast powder. Bake in jelly cake tins.

### FILLING.

One coffee cup milk, three-fourths cup sugar, one tablespoonful melted butter. When the above is nearly boiling, add three teaspoonfuls of corn starch, dissolved in a little milk, one egg, well beaten. Stir this until it boils. When cool, add one teaspoonful of vanilla, and spread between the layers of cake.
Miss Louisa Hutchison.

### Custard Cake—No. 2.

One cup sugar, three eggs, four tablespoons butter. Beat together until light, then add two teaspoonfuls of yeast powder, mixed with one and one-half cups flour. Bake in jelly pans.

### CUSTARD FOR ABOVE.

Two-thirds cup sugar, two eggs, one-half cup flour, a little salt. Beat all together, and stir into two-thirds pint of boiling milk. Be careful and have the custard thoroughly cooked. Flavor with lemon, then place between the cakes, and frost the top one. It is best the day after it is baked.

## ICING AND FILLING FOR CAKES.

### Boiled Icing.

Dissolve two pounds of sugar with eight tablespoons of water, and boil until it will rope by pouring from a spoon. Pour slowly, and stir constantly and vigorously into the beaten whites of seven eggs. Flavor to taste, and beat until white. and cool.     Mrs. McDonell.

### Chocolate Icing—No. 1.

One-fourth pound chocolate, one cup sugar, one cup new milk, one tablespoon water. Cook to a candy, and spread while warm.     Mrs. Mason Weems.

### Cold Frosting.

One egg, nine teaspoons white, pulverized sugar. Beat very thoroughly, and add one-half teaspoon cream of tartar.

### Chocolate Icing—No. 2.

Make a boiled icing, using one pound white sugar, and the whites of three eggs, beaten very stiff. After the sugar is beaten into the eggs, add, while still hot, one cup grated chocolate. This can be used for an icing or as a filling for cakes.
    Mrs. W. J. Hancock.

### Icing Made with Gelatine.

Take half a package of gelatine; put it in a vessel and pour over it about two tablespoonfuls of boiling water. When dissolved, strain, and beat in, gradually, powdered sugar sufficient to make a nice icing.     Mrs. E. C. Blake.

### Lemon Jelly—No. 1.

Dissolve one cup sugar in the juice of a large lemon, add three well-beaten eggs and a small piece of butter. Cook this until thick, stirring constantly; and when cool spread between cakes.

### Cream Filling for Cakes.

Two eggs, one cup sugar, two tablespoons corn starch, beaten well together. Boil one pint milk, and flavor. Just as the milk boils pour in the mixture, and cook until it thickens, stirring constantly. If desired, add a small piece of butter. Split open thin sponge cakes and fill with this, or spread between them as jelly.

### Lemon Icing for Cakes.

Make a boiled icing in the usual way, and flavor very strong with fresh lemon. Spread between cakes as jelly, and then ice over the top and sides. Every alternate cake spread with jelly instead of icing makes a pleasant change; or a little grated cocoanut may be added to the icing, and sprinkled on top of the cake.

### Lemon Jelly—No. 2.

Three lemons, grated and squeezed, six eggs, beaten separately, one pound sugar, one-fourth pound butter. Mix all together; put it into a vessel of hot water, and stir until thick. To be used as jelly for cake.

### Golden Sauce—With Sponge Cake.

Make a hard sauce of two cups white sugar, three-fourths cup butter; mix in it one egg, well beaten, and two tablespoons of sweet milk. Put in pitcher or bowl and set in vessel of hot water, and stir until thick. Flavor to taste. It is excellent with a little brandy.

# BRANDIED FRUITS AND PRESERVES.

### Brandy Grapes.

Do not take the grapes from the bunches, but pick free from dirt and trash. Put in the bottom of a jar a layer of grapes and a layer of sugar, and so continue until the jar is filled, then cover with good brandy.

Brandy cherries may be made in the same manner, but they must be picked from the stems and put up in glass jars.

### Brandy Peaches—No. 1.

The peaches should be fully matured, but it is better that they should be *not quite ripe*—certainly *not soft*.

The lye used in cleaning them *must be very strong*. Try the lye with an egg or a potato, as is done when making soap. If doubtful about making lye from the house ashes, buy a box of concentrated lye and prepare it as directed.

Use the best white sugar and a good article of brandy. There is a kind of liquor called by the dealers "neutral spirits," which is quite as good as brandy, and not nearly as expensive, but it is not always to be had.

Having selected the peaches—*cling-stones*—put them into the boiling lye. Do not put so many in at a time as to crowd them in the kettle, and keep the lye steadily boiling. If the lye is strong enough, the downy skin on the peaches will be seen to break in two or three minutes, or even sooner. Take them out with a strainer-dipper or a strainer-ladle and lay them into a tub of cold water, and rub each peach with a coarse towel; the skin will come off, leaving the fruit as smooth as glass. As fast as you rub off the skin lay them into another tub of cold water, until all are done.

The syrup used should be prepared before hand; fifteen

pounds of sugar will be enough for forty pounds of peaches. If it is necessary to clarify the syrup, use the whites and the shells of two eggs, boil five minutes, then strain, and boil again until you see that it is a rich syrup, but not turning again to sugar. Keep the syrup steadily boiling, lay into it as many peaches as will lie on the syrup without crowding one another—for if they crowd, they will lose their shape, and will look bruised. Very large peaches will need to boil twelve or fifteen minutes—smaller ones can be taken out in from six to ten minutes. You must watch them, and remove them as fast as you see that they seem to be cooked; you can try them with a large pin. As fast as taken out, spread them on platters to cool. When all are taken out, see that the syrup is well boiling, and put in again as many as can lie in the syrup without being crowded, and boil as before; thus do until all have been boiled.

Make a fresh syrup, allowing one pound of sugar to two pounds of fruit. Let this syrup be very clear, and boiled until it is very rich; add to it the liquor in the proportion of one measure of brandy to two measures of syrup. Place the fruit in glass jars, each jar *not more than two-thirds full;* pour on the mixture of syrup and liquor, but do not quite fill the jars; cover them air-tight, if possible, and let them so remain for five or six days. By that time some of the fruit will rise to the surface, which is caused by the juice that has been extracted; then fill up the jars to the very top with pure, strong brandy; seal them up and let them remain until Christmas.

### Brandy Peaches—No. 2.

Take fine, large, plum peaches, and peel them. Have ready a rich, white sugar syrup (boiling) into which drop the peaches. When tender enough to be pierced by a straw, skim them out on a dish, and put in the sun. Then boil the syrup down very thick. When cold, fill the jars with the peaches, sprinkling fine sugar between them. Fill the jar half full with the syrup, then add brandy until full. Seal up tight, and keep in a cold place.                              Mrs. T. W. House.

### Brandy Peaches—No. 3.

Use ripe fruit, but not sufficiently so to be soft. Make a strong soda water, using two large tablespoonfuls of soda to a gallon of water. Put this into a preserving kettle and let it boil. When boiling, put in the peaches, having first weighed them, a few at a time, turning them over in the water. Let them remain long enough for the skin to be loosened; take out, rub the skin off with a coarse towel, and throw them into cold water. If the soda water becomes too weak, add a little more soda. Make a syrup, using a pound of sugar to a pound of fruit, put the peaches in and let them scald well, remove them and continue to boil the syrup until it is quite thick. When the peaches are cold, put them in jars and cover with peach brandy, and let them remain until the next day. Pour off the syrup when it becomes sufficiently thick. After the peaches have stood for one night, pour off the brandy, add the syrup to it, stir well together and return it to the peaches.

The juice from the peaches will weaken the brandy, and it may be necessary, after a week or two, to add more. No spices should be used in putting up the fruit, but after the peaches are eaten, the syrup may be spiced, and will make excellent cordial.

Cherries, plums, damsons, grapes and pears are all good put up in the same way.

### To Can Peaches.

Make a syrup, using two pounds of sugar to six pounds of peaches, and one-half pint of water to each pound of sugar. Skim the syrup as soon as it boils, then put in the peaches and let them boil ten or fifteen minutes. Fill the cans and seal while hot.

### Peach Marmalade.

Marmalade may be made without peeling the peaches. Soft peaches are best. Cut the fruit from the stones and weigh; allow three fourths of a pound of sugar to a pound of fruit. Put the fruit into a preserving kettle, having first mashed it well—do not add water. Let the peaches boil until clear, stirring to prevent burning, then add the sugar and cook thoroughly. Put into bowls and seal like jelly. Do not strain, for if well cooked there will be no trace of the skins.

### Peach Chips.

Peel good peaches, slice very fine. Make a syrup of a half pound of sugar to a pound of fruit, and water enough to dissolve the sugar. Boil the syrup till very thick, then put in the peaches and scald well. Remove them with a perforated skimmer and dry in the sun. After they are dry, pack closely in jars, sprinkling powdered sugar between layers.

These may be used in place of raisins in fruit puddings.

### Can Peaches.

One peck peaches, five pounds sugar, one quart water. Boil the syrup until clear. In the meantime fill the cans or jars with peaches, packed as full as possible—either whole or in halves. Pour the syrup boiling hot over them; then place the jars thus filled in pans of water on the stove, and let them be heated to the boiling point—then seal.

### Ripe Tomato Preserves.

Seven pounds of tomatoes and six pounds of sugar, the juice of three lemons. Peel the tomatoes, and let all stand together over night, drain off the syrup and boil it, skimming well, then put in the tomatoes and boil gently twenty minutes. Take out the tomatoes with the skimmer, and spread on dishes to cool. Boil down the syrup until it thickens. Put preserves in jars and fill up with hot syrup.

### Preserved Peaches—No. 1.

Take one-half pound of loaf sugar to one pound fruit. Put enough water with sugar to make syrup. Drop the peaches, cut in halves into the boiling syrup, and let stay five minutes, then take out carefully on a plate; boil the syrup ten minutes, return peaches and put in glass jars and seal while boiling hot.

Pears and apples are preserved in the same way. If the fruit is not thoroughly ripe, it should be steamed or boiled until it begins to soften before putting into the syrup.

### Spiced Raisins.

Take raisins, on the stem, and boil them in water until tender. Make a syrup of one pound sugar, one-half pint good vinegar, one-half pint water; add mace, cloves and cinnamon. Boil fifteen minutes and pour over the raisins. Put in glass jars and seal while hot. They are a nice relish with cold meats or with roast turkey.

### Citron.

Cover the rind with salt water for twelve hours, then with fresh water until the salt is out; then scald in alum water; then in clear water until alum is out. Have ready a strong ginger tea and boil the rind well in that; then to one pound rind use one and one-half pounds of sugar. Use ginger and lemon for flavoring.   Mrs. B. D. Orgain, Bastrop.

### Preserved Tomatoes.

One pound of sugar to one of tomatoes. Take six pounds of each, the peel and juice of four lemons, and a quarter of a pound of ginger, tied up in a bag. Boil slowly for three hours.

### Preserved Peaches—No. 2.

Use either cling or free-stones. Peel the peaches and cut from the stones in as large pieces as possible. Allow to every three quarts of fruit one quart of sugar, and put the whole in a preserving kettle, with sufficient water to prevent the sugar scorching, put over a moderate fire and cook until the fruit is thoroughly done. Fill your jars with cold water, put them in a vessel of cold water place over the fire and bring to a boil. Have them hot when the fruit is done, pour out the boiling water, and fill at once with the fruit to within two inches from the top, then pour in about three tablespoons of whisky. Seal tight, wash the jars well, and keep in a cool place.

Mrs. D. C. Smith.

### Water Melon Rind Preserves.

Let your melon rinds stay four or five days in salt and water then change them into fresh water until they become fresh; then make a strong alum water and boil them one hour; then take them out and let them stand in fresh water until cold;

then boil in strong ginger water to flavor them. To each pound of rind add one-half pound of sugar. Boil one hour in this, then add two pounds of sugar to each pound of rind; boil two hours longer. Have plenty of water as it will boil down.

### Fig Preserves.

To each pound of fruit allow three-fourths pound of sugar. Take a sufficient number of lemons to flavor the amount of fruit you have, slice thin and simmer until soft in a little water; remove the slices and wet the sugar with the water in which the lemons were cooked, wetting the sugar only enough to prevent scorching; boil a little while, until clear syrup; put in the figs and lemon, and cook until the figs are transparent, remove the fruit and let the syrup boil down thick, then return the fruit to it and boil until all seems to be thoroughly done. Put into hot jars, seal tightly and keep in a cool place.

Mrs. W. J. Hancock.

### Fig Jam.

Weigh your fruit so as to allow three-fourths of a pound of sugar to a pound of fruit. Cut the stems from the figs, mash them well and put over the fire without water, unless the figs are too dry. When they have cooked clear, stirring to prevent burning, then add the sugar, and cook until done.

### Apple Jelly—No. 1.

Core and quarter, but not *pare*, tart apples. Cook in a little more water than will cover them until well reduced; strain, add one pound of sugar to one pint of juice. Boil twenty minutes or half an hour, then strain carefully into your molds. Slices of lemon or Jamaica ginger may be added to the apples while boiling.

### Wild Plum Jelly.

Take wild plums, green, wash them carefully and fill the kettle nearly full with the fruit, cover with cold water, let them boil until perfectly soft, then mash them with a spoon, pour into a flannel bag, and let drip, then pour in some more cold water, putting your hand into the bag, mash and stir well,

then let it drip again. Cook only two pints of the juice at a time—two pints of syrup and two pints of coffee A sugar. Let it boil fast until it will jelly on the spoon. Pour into glasses when quite hot, and set in the sun as long as convenient.
Mrs. Rob't Wilson.

### Grape Jelly.

Cover the grapes with water and boil thirty minutes, bruising them meantime with ladle until the juice runs freely; then strain through a flannel bag, and measure one pint of juice for one pound of sugar. Boil the juice fifteen or twenty minutes before putting in the sugar. After adding the sugar, let it boil five minutes.

Fruit not perfectly ripe will make the best jelly.

### Apple Jelly—No. 2.

Take apples, wipe and slice them, using skins, cores and all. Cook them soft in new cider, using enough to cover them. Strain through a cloth. Boil until the juice thickens; add a pound of sugar to a pint of juice, and boil a few minutes.

### Wild Plum Jelly.

Wild plums are best for jelly just before they ripen. To four quarts of plums add six quarts of water; let them boil until they fall to pieces, pour into a crash or flannel bag, and let the juice drip all night, until it is all strained out, then add to the juice sugar in the proportion of a pound of sugar to a pint of juice. Let it boil rapidly until it will jelly. This may be decided by taking a little in a spoon, let it cool and push it with the finger, and if it wrinkles it is done. Pour into glasses and cover. If your glasses have not covers, cut tissue paper the size of the top, wet in whisky and lay over the top of the jelly; then cut larger pieces, wet them with white of egg and seal loosely, as the paper will draw up and crack when dry.

### Wild Plum Jam.

Take the pulp that remains from the jelly, add water enough to make it soft and press through a colander thoroughly, so as to leave nothing but the seeds. Sweeten well—brown sugar may be used. Cook about fifteen or twenty minutes.

BRANDIED FRUITS AND PRESERVES.

### To Keep Green Grapes.

Take the grapes when small, before the seeds harden, pick from the stems and wash well; fill jars with them and cover with cold water. Seal tightly and they will keep fresh. Use for this purpose the Mustang grape.

# FANCY DISHES.

### Fritters—Banana.

One quart flour, two eggs, one-half teaspoon salt, two teaspoons yeast powder, sweet milk or water enough to make a stiff batter. Slice six bananas in the batter and fry in boiling lard. Mrs. A. J. Burke.

### Orange Fritters.

Make batter as above, and use four medium sized oranges instead of bananas. Peel and chop, and mix with the batter.
Mrs. A. J. Burke.

### Apple Fritters.

Use chopped apples instead of other fruit. Make the same batter and follow the same directions.
Mrs. A. J. Burke.

### Plain Fritters.

Make a batter as above, omitting the fruit. Drop from a large spoon in boiling lard, and fry them brown.
Mrs. A. J. Burke.

### Cheese Fritters.

Three tablespoons of flour, three tablespoons of cheese, one ounce of melted butter, one gill of tepid water, one egg. Put a pinch of salt in the white of the egg to make it froth quickly. Put the flour in a bowl, make a hollow in the middle, and put into it the butter, beaten yelk of the egg, the tepid water, grated cheese and pepper and salt to taste; after stirring well, add the beaten white of egg. Mrs. E. R. Falls.

### Apples for Tea.

Pare a dozen or more apples, core them carefully, and fill the centre of each apple with sugar and a small lump of butter. Put them in a pan with half pint water; baste occasionally with the syrup while baking. When done, serve with cream.

### Steamed Apples.

Have a perforated circular tin of a size to a fit in a kettle half way from the bottom. Put apples in the tin; keep the water boiling in the kettle. In one hour they will be done. Lay them in a dish and spread butter over them, then sprinkle sugar over them, a little cinnamon, nutmeg, and cover until wanted.

### Oranges—Sliced.

Peel and cut them across in slices about a quarter of an inch thick. Put a layer of these slices on the bottom of a dish and a layer of sugar over them. Continue to alternate in this way until the dish is full. Set aside until the sugar is absorbed. These are eaten at dinner, with other desserts, or at tea.

### Apple Compote.

Peel, core and halve some large apples, then boil them until tender in water with a few slices of lemon. Make a syrup of half a pound of sugar to each pound of fruit. Carefully place the apples, concave side up, on a glass dish and fill the hollow of each one with plum or currant jelly, and when the syrup is cool pour it over them.

### Apple Jam.

Stew and mash with equal quantity of sugar, and a few drops of lemon. Put in a mold, and when cold slice for tea.

### Snow Flake—No. 1.

Soak one box gelatine in one pint cold water until soft, then pour over it one quart boiling water, and add one pound sugar, the juice and grated rind of three lemons. Strain carefully through a cloth and set in a cool place. When it begins to congeal, beat hard with an egg beater for several minutes, then add the well-frothed whites of three or four eggs and beat until the whole is white and stiff. Pile high on a glass stand with small pieces of red jelly scattered over the top.

Mrs. F. C. Usher.

FANCY DISHES. 155

### Floating Island.
Take a large glass of bright jelly, whites of three eggs, well frothed, a little lemon juice, with grated peel. Beat all well together, and place in centre of a dish of cream.

### Apple Cream or Snow.
Stew some apples in water till soft, then pass them through a sieve. sweeten and flavor to taste. Beat stiff with the whisked whites of five eggs. Serve with cream.
Mrs. McDonald.

### Apple Custard.
Take tart apples; core and fill the openings with sugar and a little lemon juice. Bake until soft, then put in a dish and pour over them a custard of eggs and milk—four eggs to one quart of milk.
Mrs. F. M. Noble.

### Compote of Apples.
One pound apples, peeled and sliced, one pound sugar. Boil until the apples can be pierced with a straw. Take out the fruit, place in a deep dish, then add to the syrup one-half ounce gelatine, and boil fifteen minutes and pour over the fruit.

### Ornamental Dish.
Pare, core without splitting, some small sized tart apples, and boil gently, with one lemon for every six apples, till a straw will pass through them. Make a syrup of one-half pound white sugar for each pound of fruit, and place the apples gently into it and boil until they look clear. Take them out carefully and add to the syrup one ounce clarified isinglass; let it boil, then strain over the fruit and serve.
Mrs. G. A. McDonald.

### Apples with Jelly—For Tea.
Pare and core one dozen large apples; put in a kettle with enough boiling water to cover them, and set over the fire. Let them boil until they look as if they would break. Remove apples, and put one pound of sugar into same water, and let the syrup come to a boil. Put apples in again, and let them stay until done and clear; then slice into syrup one large lemon, and add one ounce gelatine, dissolved in one pint

cold water. Let the whole mix well and come to a boil. Arrange apples in dish to serve, and pour syrup over. Set aside until jelly congeals around the apples.

Mrs. E. H. Vincent.

### Snow Flake—No. 2.

Dissolve one-half package gelatine in one-half pint water, add one pound sugar, juice of four lemons, and whites of two eggs. Beat together until very light and spongy; then pour into molds. When eaten, serve with a custard made of the yelks of two eggs. You may omit the custard; it is nice without.

Mrs. E. H. Vincent.

### Frosted Peaches.

Twelve large, rich peaches, free-stones, whites of three eggs, whisked to a standing froth, two tablespoonfuls of water, one cup of powdered sugar. Mix water and beaten whites, dip in each peach, when you have rubbed off the fur, and roll in sugar. Set carefully on the stem end upon white paper laid in a sunny place. When half dry, roll again in sugar, expose to sun and breeze until dry, then put in a cool, dry place, until ready to use them for table.

Mrs. D. C. Smith.

### Apple Float.

Take a quart of stewed apples, press them through a sieve, sweeten and flavor to taste; then beat into them the well-frothed whites of three or four eggs. Beat well, and pile up in a glass bowl half filled with cream or rich milk.

Mrs. Noble.

### Apple Snow.

Bake six large apples. When cold, scrape the pulp, and put in a bowl with one cup of sugar and the white of an egg. Beat all to a snow.

### Solid Custard.

One box of Cox's gelatine, one gallon of milk. Let the gelatine dissolve in the milk, sweeten to taste, and let this come to a boil. Pour over the beaten yelks of ten eggs. When cool, flavor with vanilla, beat in the whites of the eggs, and mold. Serve with cream.

Miss Forman, Cynthiana, Ky.

### Lemon Meringue.

Beat the yelks of six eggs until they are thick, add the juice and grated rind of two lemons, and a cup of sugar. Place upon the stove to boil; and when the mixture begins to thicken, add the whites of the eggs, beaten till they stand alone. Line a deep dish with sponge cake, pour in the mixture and cover all with the beaten whites of two eggs, and four spoons of sugar. Brown in a quick oven.

### Boiled Custard.

Ten eggs, leaving out the whites of four, one quart of cream, Stir well together, after beating eggs separately, sweeten and flavor to taste. Boil until as thick as cream, stirring constantly. When removed from the fire, stir until nearly cold.

Mrs. B. D. Orgain, Bastrop.

### Custard.

Three eggs, three-fourths of a cup of sugar, one tablespoon of corn starch stirred into a pint of milk that has nearly boiled. When done, remove from the stove and flavor with lemon.

Agnes L. Dwight, Chicago, Ill.

### Snow Custard.

One-half package of Cox's gelatine, three eggs, one pint of milk, two cups of sugar, juice of one lemon. Soak the gelatine one hour in a teacupful of cold water; to this, then add one pint of boiling water; stir until the gelatine is thoroughly dissolved, and add two-thirds of the sugar and lemon juice. Beat the whites of the eggs to a stiff froth; and when the gelatine is quite cold, whip it into the whites, a spoonful at a time, for at least one hour. Whip steadily, and when all is stiff, pour into a mold previously wet with cold water and set in a cold place. In four hours turn into a glass dish. Make a custard of the milk, eggs and remainder of the sugar, flavor with vanilla, and when the meringue is turned out of the mold pour this around the base.

### Pineapple Cream.

Whisk up one-half pint cream quite stiff, add to this a little chopped pineapple, and the juice of one lemon, four ounces

FANCY DISHES.

powdered sugar, one ounce isinglass, dissolved in a little boiling water. Whisk lightly together and pour in a mold, and when required, dip the mold in warm water for twenty seconds. wipe with a cloth and turn on a dish. Garnish with slices of lemon and fresh flowers. A. W.

### Russian Cream.

Half a box gelatine, beaten up with the yelks of four eggs and a small cup of sugar. Put one pint of milk in a sauce-pan and set it on the stove to boil. Stir in the above mixture, and boil until like boiled custard When half cold, stir in the beaten whites of the eggs, flavor to taste, and pour in molds. This is very fine. Mrs. G. A. McDonell.

### Fruit Salad.

Alternate layers of cut fruit—bananas, oranges, pineapples, with grated cocoanut. Sprinkle white sugar over each layer of fruit.

### Spanish Float.

Make a boiled custard in the usual way, leaving out the whites of the eggs. Beat the whites slightly, and then add pulverized sugar, VERY GRADUALLY, as many tablespoons as there are eggs, beating hard all the time. Beat until very stiff, and then add, gradually, enough acid jelly to color it prettily. If the jelly is very hard, melt it before beating it in. Flavor the custard nicely, and pour in a glass dish, then pile the float on top as high as it will stand.

This makes a very ornamental dish, and when well made, is often mistaken for whipped cream.

Mrs. F. C. Usher.

### Whip Syllabub.

One quart rich cream, juice of three lemons, three-fourths pound of sugar, wine to taste. Whip all well together, and put the froth in glasses as fast as it rises.

### Spanish Cream—No. 1.

One ounce gelatine, three pints milk, six eggs, eight tablespoons sugar. Soak the gelatine one hour in the milk, then let it come to a boil; stir in the yelks well beaten, with the su

FANCY DISHES.   159

gar. Just let it simmer, stirring often to prevent burning, then pour over the well-frothed whites and mix well. Flavor with lemon.

### Spanish Cream—No. 2.

One-half box gelatine, one quart sweet milk, yelks three eggs, one small cup sugar. Soak the gelatine an hour in the milk; put on the stove and stir well as it warms. Beat the yelks very light, with the sugar, add to the scalding milk, and heat to boiling point, stirring all the time. Flavor with lemon or vanilla. Strain through muslin or tarleton, and when almost cold, pour into a mold wet with cold water.   A. W.

### Charlotte Russe—No. 1.

Whip three pints cream, sweetened and flavored to taste; whites of six eggs, well beaten. Whip the cream and skim off alternately cream and eggs and mix well. Dissolve one-half box gelatine, and stir rapidly.   A. H.

### Charlotte Russe—No. 2.

With a sharp knife, cut out smoothly the inside of a large sponge cake, leaving the bottom and sides, fill with a rich boiled custard made as follows: One pint of milk, one pint of cream, eight eggs, flavor, and mix the custard with one ounce of gelatine which has been boiled to a jelly in a little water.   Mrs. Jas. Converse.

### Charlotte Russe—No. 3.

One pint of milk made into a custard with the yelks of six eggs, sweetened with half a pound of sugar, and flavored with vanilla. Strain into the custard one ounce of isinglass dissolved in two cups of milk. When the mixture is cold, and begins to stiffen, mix with it, gradually, one pint rich cream, whipped to a froth. Put strips of sponge cake around a mold, pour the custard in, and turn out when ready to serve.

Mrs. W. A. S. Haynie.

### Whipped Cream.

One pint cream, beat until light, whites of four eggs, well frothed. Mix well, and sweeten and flavor to taste.

FANCY DISHES.

### Tipsy Squire.

Make a boiled custard in the usual way, and pour it into a bowl or deep dish. Have a sponge cake the size of the dish, and about half an inch thick. Place the cake on the custard, and over it pour half tumbler wine; then blanch one and three-fourths pounds almonds, beat them in a mortar with a little warm water, and sprinkle them over the cake. Garnish the edges with the whites of the eggs, beaten to a stiff froth.

Mrs. G. A. McDonald.

### Meringues.

One cup sugar, one cup butter, three eggs, half nutmeg. Beat the butter and sugar to a cream, add the well-beaten yelks, with enough flour to make a dough. Roll one-half inch thick, cut into cakes and bake quickly. When cool lay on each a spoonful of jelly. Then make a meringue by beating to a stiff froth the whites of the eggs, then adding one cup of powdered sugar, and spread over each cake. Place in a moderate oven, and brown slightly.

Mrs. George Bastian.

### Vanity.

Flour wet up with an egg, roll out as thin as possible in strips about a finger's length. Fry in hot lard, and sift powdered sugar over them.

### Nondescripts—No. 1.

Beat the yelks of five eggs; add flour enough to make a dough. Roll very thin, and fry in boiling lard. When done sift powdered sugar over them.

Mrs. G. A. McDonald.

### Egg Kisses—No. 1.

Whites of ten eggs, beaten to a stiff froth, one and one-half pounds powdered sugar, beaten gradually into the eggs. Flavor to taste, and beat until very light. Bake on paper, wet or slightly greased, in a moderate oven.

Mrs. F. C. Usher.

### Egg Kisses—No. 2.

Whites of six eggs, one pound pulverized sugar. Rub the

FANCY DISHES.      161

flavoring into the sugar. The eggs cannot be beaten too thoroughly; when very stiff, stir in gradually the sugar. Bake in a moderately hot oven on a board spread with wet paper. Before baking dust well with powdered sugar.

### Trifle.

Soak sponge cake in wine, and pour over it some custard. Sweeten cream, whip to a rich froth and lay on top.

### Aurora.

Beat the whites six eggs to a froth with a tablespoon of powdered sugar to each white. Beat very thoroughly, and then add, gradually, enough jelly to give it a pretty color. Whip a pint of cream, sweeten and flavor, and pour the first preparation over it and serve with nice cake.

### Nondescripts—No. 2.

Yelks of three or four eggs, beaten well; add flour enough to make a dough. Roll very thin, cut out with a tin cutter, double in the centre and fry in hot lard. Sprinkle sugar over them while hot.    Mrs. Jno. D. Rogers, Galveston.

### Wine Jelly.

One package gelatine, dissolved in one pint luke-warm water. When dissolved, add one pint boiling water, one pint sugar, one pint sherry wine, juice and grated rind of one lemon, one teaspoon ground cinnamon. Strain through a flannel bag.
Mrs. Jas. W Stacey.

### Ambrosia—No. 1.

One grated cocoanut, one can pineapples, four oranges. Cut the oranges in thin slices. Put a layer of pineapple, sprinkle a little cocoanut over, and a little sugar, a layer of oranges, and then cocoanut, and so on until finished; then pour the juice of the pineapple over.
Mrs. C. W. Hurd.

### Ambrosia—No. 2.

Is made by putting alternate layers of grated cocoanut, sliced orange and pineapple. Begin with orange, and use cocoanut last. Sprinkle sugar between each layer.

FANCY DISHES.

### Snow.

Grated cocoanut, ornamented with delicate green vines or sprays.

### Syllabub.

Beat to a solid froth the whites of four eggs, and mix with a pint of rich cream; sweeten with four tablespoonfuls of powdered sugar, add wine to taste and whip to a stiff froth. It should be whipped until very solid.

### Floating Island.

Place slices of sponge cake at the bottom of a large glass dish; pour the dish half full of rich, boiled custard. Leave out the whites of the eggs used in making the custard, and beat them to a stiff froth with six tablespoonfuls of gelatine or calf's foot jelly. Put this irregularly on top of the custard. Any kind of fruit jelly may be used in place of those mentioned, using four tablespoonfuls instead of six.

### Corn Starch Blanc Mange.

Four or five tablespoonfuls of corn starch to one quart of milk. Beat the Starch thoroughly with two eggs, and add it to the milk when near boiling, with a little salt; boil a few minutes, stirring it briskly. Flavor to taste and cool in small cups or wine-glasses. When cold and stiff, turn into a glass stand. Sweeten while cooking or use a sauce of sugar and cream.

Farina blanc mange is made in the same way.

### A Nest of Eggs.

Make blanc mange, and pour into egg shells from which the contents have been taken through a small hole in the side. Take lemon or orange peel, and, with sharp scissors, cut into shreds. Make a rich boiled custard, pour into a dish and put all around the edges of the dish the lemon peel (having boiled it tender) to make the nest; then peel the egg-shells from the blanc mange, and put the blanc mange eggs in the middle of the dish, the smooth side up.

### Preparation of Figs for Market.

Sheets are held under the trees, clear of the ground, and the fruit shaken into them. They are then placed in baskets and dipped in a bath of strong potash lye for two minutes, and then dipped in clear water. This is to remove the gum on the outside of the fruit, and to improve the color. Dry them in the sun, and pack carefully in boxes.

### Macaroons.

Pour boiling water over half a pound of sweet almonds, and rub off the skins. Wipe them dry, and then pound them fine in a mortar, adding rosewater to taste. Beat the whites of three eggs to a stiff froth; stir in gradually a pound of white sugar, then the almonds, and mix well. Bake in a moderate oven, in small cakes, slightly separated, with powdered sugar sifted over each one.

### Sugar Candy—No. 1.

Two cups sugar, one-half cup water, one tablespoon butter, two tablespoons vinegar.

Mrs. J. D. Sayers, Bastrop, Texas.

### Butter Scotch.

One cup sugar, one cup molasses, one cup butter. Boil until brittle.

### Cocoanut Candy—No. 1.

Take one quart white sugar, with enough water to dissolve it. While boiling, stir continually; and when it thickens, mix in one grated cocoanut, sprinkling a little of the latter on top when nearly cold.

### Chocolate Caramels—No. 1.

Two cups sugar, one cup warm water, one-half cup grated chocolate, three-fourths cup butter. Let it boil without stirring until it snaps in water.

### Chocolate Candy.

Take two pounds coffee sugar; wet it with water, and add one tablespoon of vinegar. Have greased two dishes, in one of which grate one stick chocolate. Boil the candy until it will rope, and then pour half in the empty dish and the rest over the chocolate. When cool enough, work the latter lightly with the fingers; at the same time, having some one to pull the other very white. Lay one kind over the other, and let it cool. Mrs. G. A. Gibbons.

### Chocolate Caramels—No. 2.

One-half pint of milk; let it boil, and add to it two grated cakes of chocolate, then add one-half pint of molasses and four tablespoons of sugar. Flavor with vanilla, and boil constantly and fast until done, but be careful not to burn.
Mrs. E. C. Atkinson.

### Cream Chocolate Drops.

Take two cups white sugar, one cup cold water, one-half pound chocolate. Let the sugar and water boil together ten or twelve minutes, then take off and beat rapidly, until it is light and creamy, flavor with vanilla. Place the chocolate where it will melt slowly into a paste, then roll little balls of the cream (a teaspoonful to one ball) into the paste, and cool on buttered tins. Mrs. O'Donoghue, Chicago.

### Cocoanut Candy—No. 2.

Two and one-half pounds coffee A sugar, with one cup and a half of water poured over it and cooked rapidly until it will sugar again, which may be known by putting a small quantity on a plate and stirring it. One pound grated cocoanut spread on a large dish; over this the boiling syrup is then poured and stirred until it sugars sufficiently to put in cakes on buttered plates. If it sugars too rapidly, stir in a small quantity of water. Mrs. Rob't Brown, Navasota, Texas.

### Peanut Candy.

Take four cups sugar and moisten it with water and three tablespoonsful vinegar. When it boils, put in a piece of butter the size of an egg and cook until it becomes brittle. Have the peanuts parched and shelled in a buttered dish, and pour over them the syrup. Beat lightly with a fork or egg-beater until stiff.

### Prauliens.

Make syrup as for the above, leaving out the butter, and pour over pecans, carefully shelled and picked over, stirring rapidly until stiff.

### Black Crook Candy.

One pint molasses, one-half pint brown sugar, one pound prepared cocoanut. Boil until it candies.

Mrs. Ella O'Donoghue, Chicago.

### Cocoanut Candy—No. 3.

Grate one cocoanut and dry. Take one and one-half pounds white sugar, wet it with water, and boil it until it is brittle. Have ready the whites of two eggs, beaten to a stiff froth; pour the boiling syrup over them, beat well and add the cocoanut. Beat until it whitens, then pour into a greased dish, and when cold cut into cakes. Mrs. O. H. Hutchison.

### Cocoanut Candy—No. 4.

Boil one-half pound loaf sugar with one-half teacup water. Stir in one-half pound grated cocoanut, flavor with lemon, and pour in buttered tins. Mrs. O'Donoghue.

### Cocoanut Candy—No. 5.

Take one cocoanut, peel and cut in thin slices, and spread thickly in a greased dish. Make syrup same as for chocolate candy, and boil very hard; pour over cocoanut, and when cold cut in squares. Mrs. G. A. Gibbons.

### [Cream Candy—No. 1.

Four cups sugar, two cups water, three-fourths cup vinegar, one cup cream or rich milk, piece of butter size of an egg, a pinch of soda, flavor with vanilla. Let it boil until it cracks in water, then work white.

### Cream Candy—No. 2.

Two cups granulated sugar, one-half cup water, one teaspoon vanilla, one tablespoon vinegar, small piece of butter. Boil it, but do not stir; try it in water, and when brittle pour in buttered plates.

### Sugar Candy—No. 2.

Three tumblers good brown or white sugar, one and one-half tumblers cold water, one tablespoon good vinegar and a small teaspoon butter. Boil without stirring until it begins to rope. To pull, begin as soon as it can be handled, and take hold only with the tips of fingers. Pull rapidly—use very little grease on the hands.

### Molasses Candy.

One cup molasses, one-half cup sugar, one tablespoon vinegar, butter the size of a walnut. Boil twenty minutes, stirring constantly. When done, add a pinch of soda, and stir briskly. Pour in buttered tins, and when cool pull it.

Mrs. Ellen O'Donoghue, Chicago.

### Chocolate Cream Drops.

One cake of vanilla chocolate, three cups of powdered sugar, one cup of soft water, two tablespoons corn starch or arrowroot, one tablespoonful butter, two teaspoons vanilla. Wash from the butter all the salt, stir the sugar and water together, mix in the corn starch, bring to a boil, stirring constantly; boil about ten minutes and add the butter. Take from the fire and beat until it looks like cream. Roll into balls and lay on a greased dish. Grate fine the chocolate, put it into a sauce-pan and melt by putting the pan in boiling water. When it melts, beat smooth, with two tablespoons of powdered sugar, and roll the cream balls in it. Dry on a cold dish.

### Cream Nuts.

Use pecans or English walnuts. Remove the shells, taking care not to break the halves. Make a cream of the following: Two cups of sugar, one cup of water, one and a half tablespoons of arrowroot, flavor to taste. Boil about five or ten minutes, stirring all the time, then beat up until like thick cream. With your hands roll into balls like a marble and press the halves of the nuts into two sides of the ball.

Mrs. W. J. Hancock.

# WINES AND BEVERAGES.

### Dewberry Wine.

To every three pints of berries add one quart of water; suffer it to stand twenty-four hours, strain through a colander, then through a jelly-bag, and to every gallon of juice add three pounds of loaf sugar. Put in a stone jug, filled up, and kept full with some of the same juice reserved for that purpose, until it stops fermenting, which will be in two or three weeks. Cork it tightly, and keep it in a cold place for three or four months, then pour it off into bottles, cork and seal close. If the wine is kept for twelve months it will be better, and will continue to improve with age.

Miss Dunovant, Eagle Lake.

### Blackberry Wine—No. 1.

One gallon of berries, pour over one quart of boiling water, add two and one-half (2½) pounds of sugar. Let it stand ten days, then strain and bottle it.

### Blackberry Wine—No. 2.

Measure your berries and bruise them. To every gallon, add a quart of boiling water. Let the mixture stand twenty-four hours, stirring occasionally; then strain off the liquid into a cask, to every gallon adding two pounds of sugar. Cork tightly, and let stand until the following October, and you will have wine ready for use without further straining or boiling. It may be improved by adding a little pure French brandy, and perhaps keep better.

### Scuppernong Wine.

Mash the grapes, squeeze out all the juice and strain. To every gallon of juice, add two pounds of white sugar. Let it stand twenty-four hours, then put it in a vessel to ferment. When fermentation ceases, cork it slightly at first, afterwards make it tight. It will be ready to bottle it three or four months.

Mrs. W. A. S. Haynie.

### Blackberry Wine—No. 3.

Fill large stone jars with ripe black or dewberries, cover them with water, mash, and let them stand several hours, then strain through a thick cloth, and add three pounds of white sugar to every gallon of juice. Let the wine stand a few days, stirring and skimming each day, then put in a demijohn, but do not cork it up for some time.

Mrs. W. A. S. Haynie.

### Mustang Grape Wine.

Gather the grapes perfectly ripe. Have ready a molasses or whisky barrel with the head out. Put in the grapes, and mash them well. Let them stand one week. Then bore a hole in the barrel about eight inches from the bottom. Draw off into a tub, straining through a thick blanket; sweeten the grape juice with sugar (brown will answer) until it will float an egg. Put into jugs, a thin cloth tied over the top, let them stand in a cool place to ferment. As soon as it is done fermenting cork tightly.

After standing two or three months it will be much improved by drawing off and put into bottles, and putting a raisin or two in each bottle. In drawing off avoid shaking as much as possible.

R. M. Fenn.

### Blackberry Cordial—No. 1.

To one gallon of blackberries add one half gallon of water. Boil until well cooked, then strain through a flannel bag, add to the juice one pound of sugar, two teaspoons of ground spice, two of cloves, two of powdered cinnamon and one grated nutmeg. Boil until thick, take from the fire, and, when cool, add one quart of brandy or whisky. Bottle and cork tightly, and it will keep for years.

Mrs. J. Hill, Bastrop.

### Blackberry Cordial—No. 2.

Stem the berries, strain the juice, and to every pint of juice add one-half pint of loaf sugar. Tie in a thin cloth, cloves and spice to flavor, boil all together until thick and rich. When cool, add one-half pint of brandy to each quart of juice. Bottle closely.  Mrs. T. W. House.

### Blackberry Cordial—No. 3.

To every quart of juice allow one pound of loaf sugar boiled to a thin jelly. When cold, to every quart of juice allow a quart of brandy. Add spices to taste, then bottle up.

Mrs. T. C. Armstrong.

### Ginger Beer.

Two ounces of ginger to a pint of molasses; add a gallon of warm water, stir it well; add one-half pint of yeast.

### Cream Nectar.

Six pounds of loaf sugar, four ounces tartaric acid, two quarts water. Warm this mixture, and add the whites of four eggs, beaten to a froth. Be careful not to let it boil. When cool, strain and add a teaspoon of essence of lemon.

*Directions for Use.*—Take two tablespoons of the above syrup to a glass two-thirds full of water and add a small quantity of carbonate of soda, stir until it effervesces—drink.

### Imperial Lemonade.

Half a lemon, one tablespoon pulverized white sugar, one tablespoon pineapple, cut fine, one tablespoon strawberries, one peach, cut fine, fill up the glass with pounded ice and mix well.

### Milk Punch.

Two tablespoons of brandy, into six tablespoons of sweet milk, and add two tablespoons of white sugar, and, if liked, grate a little nutmeg over it.

# ICES.

### Lemon Ice.

To one quart strong lemonade, made very sweet, add beaten whites of six eggs and freeze. L. BARRETT.

### Lemon Sherbet.

Two pounds sugar, eight lemons, four quarts water. Strain carefully and freeze. A can of finely chopped pineapple may be added to this if desired.

### Italian Cream.

Two pints cream, two cups sugar, two lemons, juice and grated rind, two tablespoons brandy. Mix well, stirring in the lemon very gradually, and freeze.

### Frozen Custard.

Make a boiled custard of the yelks of five eggs to a quart of milk, and sweeten and flavor to taste. When ready to freeze, beat the whites of the eggs to a stiff froth and stir into the freezer.

### Frozen Peaches.

Peel and pass through a colander very soft free-stone peaches, and sweeten. Have in your freezer an equal quantity of cream also sweetened, and when it begins to freeze add the fruit and freeze hard. The peaches may be chopped fine if preferred. Milk may be substituted for cream if necessary.

### Cocoanut Cream.

Partially freeze one gallon sweetened cream, and then add one or more grated cocoanuts, according to taste, and freeze hard.

### Frozen Whipped Cream.

One quart of cream, beaten until light, mixed with whites of four eggs well beaten. Sweeten and flavor to taste and freeze.

This makes a delicious dessert when it is prepared in this manner without freezing—simply letting it stand in ice until very cold all through.

### Strawberry Cream.

Have the cream sweetened, and, when beginning to freeze, add an equal amount of strawberries.

### Wine Sherbet.

Make a sangaree of the wine preferred, mix with the well beaten white of an egg or two and freeze.

### Strawberry Ice.

The juice of ripe strawberries sweetened to taste. Strain carefully and freeze.

### Water Melon Ice.

Select a very ripe and red melon. Scrape some of the pulp and use all the water. A few of the seeds interspersed will add greatly to its appearance. Sweeten to taste and freeze. If wished very light, add the whites of three eggs, thoroughly whipped, to one gallon of the mixture just as it begins to congeal. Beat in very hard.

Miss Forman, Cynthiana, Ky.

### Gelatine Ice.

Let one ounce of sparkling gelatine stand one hour in a pint of cold water, then add three pints of boiling water, one and a half pounds loaf sugar, one and a half pints of wine, juice of three lemons and rinds of two. Stir well and freeze before it hardens.

Miss Forman.

### Wine Ices.

Are made by taking as much lemonade as is required for freezing, making it not quite so strong as for lemon sherbet, omitting one lemon, and adding claret or sherry to taste.

By adding Jamaica rum to the lemonade instead of wine you will have Roman punch. Freeze or use ice in it.

### Milk Sherbet.

Two quarts sweet milk, four lemons, four cups sugar, one pint water, two tablespoons corn starch. Squeeze juice of lemons in the sugar. Put peel of lemons with pint of water on the fire and let simmer a few minutes, then pour the liquid on the sugar. Scald the milk with corn starch and one cup of the sugar. When cold, put in freezer, and when it begins to stiffen, add the syrup of lemon and sugar, then freeze hard.

Mrs. J. W. Jones.

# MISCELLANEOUS RECEIPTS.

### Measures for Housekeepers.

One quart wheat flour makes one pound.
One quart soft butter makes one pound.
One quart broken loaf sugar makes one pound.
One quart best brown sugar makes one pound, two ounces.
One quart white sugar powdered, makes one pound, one ounce.
Ten eggs make one pound.
Sixteen large tablespoonfuls make one-half pint.
Eight large tablespoonfuls make one gill.
Common sized tumbler holds one-half pint.
Sixty drops make one teaspoonful.

### To Prevent Mildew on Preserves.

Take the white of an egg, and wet slightly both sides of a piece of paper large enough to cover the top of the preserves. It will keep them free from mold or spoiling for two years.

Another way is to wet in alcohol papers size of jars and lay over top of preserves.

### Japanese Cleaning Cream.

One ounce castile soap, one ounce ammonia, one-half ounce glycerine, one-half ounce spirits of wine, one-half ounce ether. Put all in a quart bottle and fill with rainwater.

It will not spot the most delicate colors. Is excellent to remove spots from black goods.

Mrs. H. L. Carmer.

### Cologne Water.

To one quart of alcohol add sixty drops of lavender, sixty drops of bergamot, sixty drops of essence of lemon, sixty drops of orange water, sixty drops of attar of roses.

Mrs. A. L. Lacey.

In a few weeks it will have the appearance and flavor of pure wine of the best kind, and, mixed with water, is a delightful beverage for the sick. No alcohol is needed to preserve it.

The medical properties of the tomato are in high repute, and it is supposed that this syrup retains all that is contained in the fruit.

### Beef Tea.

Take one pound of good, juicy, tender beef; *cut* in small pieces, add half pint of water. Put in four drops only of muriatic acid. Let this stand cold three hours, then bring it to a mild heat—*never boil*. Let this stand seven hours longer. It is then ready to strain and use.

*Dose.*—Half teacup, or more or less, according to the strength of the person, Mrs. James Bailey.

### To Make Beef Tea Quickly.

Take a beefsteak, cut it into small pieces, broil them slightly and squeeze through a lemon squeezer until the juice in extracted. Season, and take while hot.

Is quite as efficacious, and more palatable than other beef tea, having more the taste of broiled steak.

### To Remove Ink Stains.

Soda will remove ink stains from the fingers, from clothing, from marble, also white spots on furniture caused by heat.

### To Clean Brushes and Combs.

Make a strong soda water into which lay your combs and brushes with bristles down. Leave them for a few hours. You will find them perfectly clean. Shake the water well from them; lay them in an airy place.

### To Clean Brushes.

Put a few drops of ammonia in water. Rub this through the brush bristles with your hand. Shake well, and dry in the open air.

Ink stains may be removed from matting by using soda and water. The soda will turn the matting yellow, but washing with strong vinegar will remove this.

two firm braids, then the roots rubbed with a sponge dipped in lukewarm sage tea, after which the braids can be washed and dried with a towel.

This preserves the color of the hair, and keeps the scalp clean.

### Simple Remedy for Three Dangerous Diseases.

A *large* onion poultice was applied to the stomach and bowels of a typhoid fever patient who had not slept for fourteen days, and had become insane. In a short time the patient dropped into a profound sleep and profuse perspiration, and soon recovered.

This *large* onion poultice is equally good in typhoid-pneumonia, if applied to the chest; and in pleurisy, if applied to the side.

A poultice of pounded peach leaves placed upon a wound soon as received will prevent lockjaw.

Nothing better to apply to burns than cooking soda. Also good for the sting of an insect.

Rub chapped hands with finely powdered starch, or beeswax and melted tallow with a little sweet oil.

Water is as good a liniment, poultice or plaster as anything you can get. Keeping the skin warm and moist is the main thing, and a wet cloth covered with a dry one will do that.

### A Good Liniment.

Equal parts of Iodide of ammonia and chloroform. Rub on the affected part.  Mrs. Wm. Christian.

### Blackberry Syrup—For Summer Complaint.

Two quarts of blackberry juice, one pound of loaf sugar, half an ounce of nutmegs, a quarter of an ounce of cloves, half an ounce of cinnamon, half an ounce of allspice. Pulverize the spice, and boil all for fifteen or twenty minutes. When cold, add a pint of brandy.

### Tomato Syrup.

Express the juice of ripe tomatoes, and put a pound of sugar to each quart of the juice. Put it in bottles and set it aside.

Blood stains may be removed from carpets or other materials not washable by applying wet starch. Put it on quite thick, and let it remain until it dries; brush it off, and if the stain has not altogether disappeared apply a second time.

### To Clean Windows.

Take a damp cloth, dip it either in whiting or prepared chalk, and rub it on the window-glass. Let it remain until dry, then rub off with a dry cloth. It is very easily and quickly done, and makes the windows very nice.

The same is excellent for cleaning mirrors.

### To Clean Pots.

Having poured out the contents, set the pot on the stove and pour in about a teacup of corn meal. Let this get hot, take a dry cloth and rub it around. The pot will be perfectly clean.

Mrs. E. Reid, Corsicana.

### Preventive for Asthma.

Take a teaspoonful of sulphur every morning before breakfast.

### Cure for Toothache.

Fill the cavity with a mixture of salt and soda.

### To Wash Blue Woolen Goods.

Use water beaten to a lather with yelk of egg instead of soap.

### To Remove Fruit Stains.

Pour boiling water over the fresh stain before washing.

### To Destroy Cut Worms in Gardens.

Throw over the plants indigo water of the strength used in washing clothes.

The above was discovered by accident in using the rinsing water for the garden in time of drought. Thinking, perhaps, the death of the worms was due to some other cause, it was repeatedly tried, thoroughly tested, and found to be their sure destruction. Mrs. M. H. Bozeman, Hempstead, Tex.

### Cleaning Woolen Clothes.

Spirits of ammonia, two ounces; spirits of ether two ounces; glycerine, two ounces; spirits of wine, two ounces; white castile soap, one-fourth of an ounce; two quarts boiling water. Dissolve the soap in the water, stirring carefully. As soon as it is cool, *i. e.* tepid, add the other ingredients. Cork carefully, and 'tis ready for use.

Rub the spots with a soft brush; in very fine materials, as merino, use a piece of the goods to rub with. If you choose, you can use a sponge. After rubbing, put the garment in the sun for an hour. If the first rubbing does not remove the stain, the second will.

### Prickly Heat.

Prickly heat may be alleviated by washing with strong soda or salt water, then wipe off perfectly dry. Or rub the affected part with dry cornmeal.

### To Clean Kid Gloves.

Use puroline, pouring sufficient into a bowl to clean the gloves, put them into the puroline and wash, rubbing hard enough to remove all dirt. When this is done, put them on the hands and dry.

### To Remove Spots from Kid Gloves.

Get a little gum ammonia, sprinkle in the bottom of a box, lay a paper over it and put in the spotted gloves, cover the box tightly, and in a day or two all the spots will have disappeared.

This has been tested, and a pair of gloves so badly spotted that none of the original color remained were found to be completely restored.

## W. H. PALMER,

(Successor to E. Milby,)

*WHOLESALE*

## Grocer and Commission Merchant,

34 and 36 Travis Street,

HOUSTON, - - - TEXAS.

---

## Ulmann, Lewis & Co.
## WHOLESALE GROCERS,

— AND —

### COTTON FACTORS,

29 and 31 Travis Street,

HOUSTON, - - TEXAS.

---

## H. D. TAYLOR

### *COTTON FACTOR,*

— AND —

## STORAGE AND COMMISSION.

Commerce Street,

HOUSTON, - - TEXAS.

---

## M. D. CONKLIN & CO.,

Successors to R. Cotter & Co.

## Wholesale and Retail Druggists,

54 Main Street, HOUSTON, TEX.

PROPRIETORS AND MANUF'RS OF

*I. X. L. Chill Cure, I. X. L. Horse Powder, I. X. L. Liver Pills, I. X. L. Liniment, I. X. L. Magic Relief, I. X. L. Sarsap. and Pot.*

Pure Extract Jamaica Ginger, Flavoring Extracts.

**TOOTH POWDER, PURE SEIDLITZ POWDERS,**

*I. X. L. Cement, Triumph Mexican Chewing Gum, Lemon Sugar, &c.*

## The R. Cotter Drug and Medicine Manf'g Co.
(WM. GINNUTH.)

## WHOLESALE DRUGGISTS.

—DEALERS IN—

DRUGS, PATENT MEDICINES, DRUGGISTS' SUNDRIES,
*Toilet and Fancy Articles.*

### SHOW CASES AT MANUFACTURERS' PRICES.

PROPRIETORS OF

Cotter's Chill Cure, Cotter's Headache Pills, Cotter's Sarsaparilla, Cotter's Cherry Cordial, Cotter's Cholera Specific, Cotter's New Liniment, Cotter's Liver Pills, Etc.

*P. O. Box No. 327.*     HOUSTON, TEXAS.

---

## ALF. CHIMENE,
Manufacturer of and Dealer in

### FURNITURE, CARPETS, MATTINGS,
Parlor Sets, Window Shades,

**No. 73 Main Street,** - - - **HOUSTON, TEXAS.**

---

## GEORGE KIDD,
### FRUIT AND PRODUCE COMMISSION MERCHANT,
*120 Main Street, HOUSTON, TEXAS.*

---

## JOHN ACHENBACH,
MANUFACTURER OF

### FINE BOOTS AND SHOES,
—AND DEALER IN—

LADIES', GENTS' AND CHILDREN'S BOOTS, SHOES, &C.
*STORE AND FACTORY,*

103 Congress St., opp. Court House,     HOUSTON, TEX.

---

## *M. MELLINGER & BRO.*
STAPLE AND

# FANCY GROCERS.

IMPORTERS AND DEALERS IN

### WINES, LIQUORS, ALES,
*AND PORTER,*

**89 and 91 Prairie St., HOUSTON, TEX.**

PROMPT ATTENTION PAID TO ALL ORDERS.

### For Felon.

Cut a lemon and keep the finger in it for twenty-four hours. Or, put unslaked lime in soft soap, make about the consistency of putty. Put the finger in while slaking. A fresh oyster applied to a felon is often a good change.

### Bread and Milk Poultice.

Put bread and milk in a cup and let it boil. Apply when warm. Good for inflammation.

### Remedy for a Burn.

Apply sweet oil immediately. Scrape the inside of a raw Irish potato, lay some of it on the burn, securing it with a cloth. In a short time put on a fresh potato. Repeat application frequently. It will give immediate ease and draw out the fire.

### Remedy for a Sore.

Mix cornmeal with charcoal and apply to the sore. It is healing as well as cleansing.

For mortification, add two tablespoons of brewers' yeast and some pounded ice.

### Remedy for Diarrhœa.

One ounce tincture of capsicum, one ounce tincture of paregoric.

*Dose.*—One tablespoon, repeated until running off ceases.

### Cholera Mixture.

Also a good remedy for diarrhœa or cramps in the stomach. Camphor gum, one drachm; paregoric one drachm; tincture catechu, one drachm; tincture ginger, two ounces; tincture cloves, one ounce; oil of peppermint, sixty drops; prepared chalk, two drachms; tincture cayenne pepper, two drachms. Mix.

*Dose.*—One teaspoon in sweetened water.

### To Cure Toothache.

The worst toothache or neuralgia resulting from the teeth may be speedily cured by the application of a bit of cotton saturated in a solution of ammonia.

### Liniment.

One ounce of chloroform, one-half ounce essence of peppermint, one-half ounce pain killer.

This is an excellent liniment for rheumatism, and, in fact, all kinds of aches and pains.

Mrs. Wm. Christian.

For bowel consumption, indigestion, diarrhœa or summer complaint, take common charcoal powdered, sift, dissolve a little in whisky, add water and sugar.

Take as often as required.

### Cure for Dyspepsia.

One ounce muriate of ammonia, one ounce gum extract of dandelion, one-half ounce of gentian root. Dissolve in three pints of cold water.

Shake well. Take tablespoonful three times a day. In extreme cases take oftener.

### Worth Knowing.

To neutralize any poison, mineral or vegetable, taken intentionally or by accident, swallow two gills of sweet oil—for a strong constitution, more oil.

### Remedy for Ague.

When the chill is at its height, the person must go to bed; let another person dip a piece of flannel, large enough to cover the bowels, in cold brandy—don't wring out the flannel—spread it on the table, dust it over with pepper out of the castor, then spread over the bowels, pepper side down. Give at the same time half a wine-glass of brandy, in which half a teaspoon of the pepper has been mixed.

This never fails to cure.

### Remedy for Ivy or Vine Poisoning.

Apply hot water, either by immersion or wet cloths, as soon as the irritation is felt. Repeat whenever the itching returns. No drugs need be used.

### Head Wash.

Sage tea is one of the best washings and dressings for the head. The hair should be carefully brushed and braided in

## N. A. BLAKE,
— DEALER IN —
### Dry Goods, Notions, Novelties, Etc.,
119 MAIN STREET, (Masonic Temple,)

SEND FOR SAMPLES.      HOUSTON, TEX.

---

## O. C. DREW,
— DEALER IN —
### STAPLE AND FANCY GROCERIES
No. 91 Main Street, HOUSTON, TEXAS.

---

## R. W. McLIN & CO.
### Dry Goods and Ladies' Furnishing Goods
67 MAIN STREET, HOUSTON, TEXAS.

---

Photography in all its branches executed from miniature to life size, in India ink, Crayon or Oil Painting. Special attention given to copies, both restoring and enlarging. Also, keep constantly on hand large assortment of Frames. Satisfaction guaranteed.

## CHAS. J. WRIGHT,
**PHOTO-ARTIST,**

Sole Licensee for the Celebrated Lambertype Permanent Photograph Patent.     HOUSTON, TEXAS.

---

☛ FINEST LINE OF GOODS IN THE STATE. ☚

### SWEENEY & COOMBS,
— DEALERS IN —

**Diamonds, Gold and Silver Watches, Gold Wedding Rings, Gold Set Rings, Bracelets, Earrings and Brooches.**

A Complete Assortment of Spectacles. Fine Watch and Jewelry Repairing a Prominent Feature.   **61 Main Street, HOUSTON, TEX.**

---

## N. T. AYRES,
Manufacturer and Dealer in

### ✶→ FINE SHOES ←✶
(MASONIC TEMPLE,)

MAIN STREET,     —    —    —     HOUSTON, TEXAS.

---

J. S. SHERWOOD.     JNO. W. BREITLING.     F. A. BREITLING, JR.

## SHERWOOD & BREITLING,
### FURNITURE AND HOUSE FURNISHING GOODS,
CARPETS, MATTING, FANCY GOODS, ETC.,

Grainger Building, No. 83 Main Street,      HOUSTON, TEXAS.

L. M. JONES & CO.,
**Wholesale and Retail Clothiers,**
BOOTS AND SHOES,
HOUSTON, — — — — TEXAS.

---

C. CONRADI,
OPTICIAN,
WATCHMAKER AND JEWELER,
67 Main Street, HOUSTON, TEXAS.

---

**TEXAS LAMP & OIL CO.**
Wholesale Dealers in
GLASSWARE, LAMPS, CHIMNEYS,
Burners, Chandeliers, Oil Stoves, Etc.
ALL BRANDS OF OILS CONSTANTLY ON HAND.
75 Main Street, HOUSTON, TEXAS.

**MILLS**
ONE PRICE CASH CLOTHIER
HOUSTON, TEXAS.

---

☞ YOUNG RELIABLE. ☜
COMMINGE & GEISLER,
— AGENTS FOR —
*NEW HOME SEWING MACHINES,*
ATTACHMENTS, NEEDLES, OIL, &c.

---

JERRY L. MITCHELL, Agt.,
*DEALER IN FINE JEWELRY*
REPAIRING A SPECIALTY.
HOUSTON, TEXAS.

---

**SAM BROS.**
CLOTHIERS, HATTERS, GENTS' FURNISHERS,
— AND —
BOOT AND SHOE DEALERS,
HOUSTON, TEXAS.

## MRS. A. BENTLEY,
## FASHIONABLE MILLINER AND FANCY GOODS,
### 71 Main Street. - HOUSTON, TEXAS.

HAVE ALWAYS ON HAND A COMPLETE STOCK OF

### Hats, Flowers, Feathers, Ornaments, Silks, Ribbons,
*Velvets, Ruchings, Collarettes, Ties, Crape, Veilings, Etc.*

Also, a full line of Zephyr Worsted of all desirable shades, Canvas, Mottoes, Card Board, Hair Goods, Switches, Braids, Frizzes, Hair Ornaments, Stamped Goods, Yokes, Bands, Pillow Shams, etc.

Stamping of all kinds done to order. Orders from the country promptly attended to, and Goods sent C. O. D. with privilege of exchanging if they do not suit.

---

## BOTTO CANDY MANUF'G CO.
### Cor. Texas Avenue and Main Street,

**SEND FOR PRICE LIST.**     **HOUSTON, TEX.**

---

### PEREIRA & RANDOLPH,
*Cor. Preston and Fannin Sts., opp. Post House,*   **HOUSTON, TEXAS.**

IMPORTERS AND DEALERS IN

## PAINTS, OILS, GLASS AND WALL PAPER

Manufacturers of Ready Mixed Paint. Agents for Murphey's Varnishes and John L. Whiting's Patent Brushes.

---

# THE TEXAS COOK BOOK.

*A Practical Work on the Art of Cookery.*

# FOR SALE BY ALL BOOKSELLERS.

### Sent Post Paid on Receipt of Price, $1.50.

## E. ERLENMEYER,

### ANALYTICAL
## CHEMIST AND PHARMACIST,

*Renders his services by advising in Chemical proceedings in kitchen and household, and recommends his Superior*

Disinfectant, Thymol Ozon, Erasive Saponine, Rat and Roach Poison, Bed Bug Poison, Cement, Indelible Ink, Furniture Polish, Lone Star Blacking, Infallible Corn Destroyer, Sozodont Tooth Ache Drops, Philocome Hair Oil, Philodont Tooth Powder, Cologne, Whooping Cough Mixture, Etc.

*ALL ARTICLES TO BE RELIED ON.*

---

C. C. WIGGIN.            B. C. SIMPSON.

## WIGGIN & SIMPSON,
### *PHŒNIX*
## IRON WORKS,

*Engineers, Founders and Machinists,*

Preston Street,           HOUSTON, TEX.

---

## E. F. SCHMIDT,
## Druggist & Apothecary.

KEEPS CONSTANTLY ON HAND A FULL ASSORTMENT OF
Drugs, Chemicals, Medicines, Patent Medicines, Sponges, Perfumeries, Toilette Articles, Mineral Waters, &c. Prescriptions carefully prepared, day and night.

66 Travis Street,          HOUSTON, TEX

---

### CHINA HALL.
## JAMES F. DUMBLE,
## China Dinner and Tea Sets,
### *FINE GLASS WARE,*
**LAMPS AND CHANDELIERS, FINE TABLE CUTLERY,**
*Plated Ware, Toys and Fancy Goods,*
Sign of Big Pitcher, 48 Main Street,
HOUSTON, TEX.

**A FIFTY DOLLAR GUARANTEE ON EVERY MATTRESS.**

## HOUSTON
# MACHINE MATTRESS FACTORY

### J. W. CRAWFORD, Proprietor.

Orders for all kinds of Mattresses, Pillows, Etc., either singly or in car load lots filled at short notice. Write for price list and be convinced of my superior goods and low prices.

**OFFICE AND FACTORY:**

**140 and 142 Congress Street, HOUSTON, TEX.**

---

| NAILS, BELTING, MILL SUPPLIES, And BRASS STEAM FITTINGS. | **GEORGE DUMBLE,** **Hardware Merchant,** 37 MAIN STREET, HOUSTON, TEXAS. | TRAVELER, GLENWOOD, ORIGINAL BUCK and TIMES **Cook Stoves** |

*— AGENT FOR —*

**DISSTON'S SAWS AND TOOLS, ALSO FAIRBANKS STANDARD SCALES.**

---

## *THOS. R. FRANKLIN,*

### FANCY & STAPLE DRY GOODS,

#### HOUSTON, TEXAS.

*SAMPLES MAILED WHEN REQUESTED AND COUNTRY ORDERS SATISFACTORILY FILLED.*

---

# H. WADDELL,

*— DEALER IN —*

# FURNITURE, CARPETS,

### AND HOUSE FURNISHING GOODS,

### 30 & 32 Main St., HOUSTON, TEX.